Communist
Revolutionary Warfare

COMMUNIST REVOLUTIONARY WARFARE

From the Vietminh to the Viet Cong

George K. Tanham

Foreword by Michael A. Sheehan

PSI Classics of the Counterinsurgency Era

Praeger Security International
Westport, Connecticut • London

Library of Congress Cataloging-in-Publication Data

Tanham, George K.
Communist revolutionary warfare : from the Vietminh to the Viet Cong / George K.
Tanham; Foreword by Michael A. Sheehan.
    p. cm. — (PSI Classics of the Counterinsurgency Era)
  Includes bibliographical references and index.
  ISBN 0–275–99263–2 (alk. paper)—ISBN 0–275–99264–0 (pbk : alk. paper)
  1. Vietnam —History   2. Guerrilla warfare 3. Communism—Vietnam.   I. Title
  II. Series
DS557.A5T3   1967
959.7'04   67021379

British Library Cataloguing in Publication Data is available.

Library of Congress Catalog Card Number: 67021379
ISBN: 0–275–99263–2
      0–275–99264–0 (pbk.)

First published in 1961

Praeger Security International, 88 Post Road West, Westport, CT 06881
An imprint of Greenwood Publishing Group, Inc.
www.praeger.com

Printed in the United States of America

The paper used in this book complies with the
Permanent Paper Standard issued by the National
Information Standards Organization (Z39.48–1984).

10 9 8 7 6 5 4 3 2 1

CONTENTS

FOREWORD

George Tanham was among the very first American students of the counterinsurgency era in the 1950s and 1960s. An artillery officer in World War II, he went on to earn a doctorate in military history and political science. This combination of experience and knowledge served him well in analyzing the rise of guerrilla warfare as it rapidly became a preoccupation for the United States. Tanham knew that insurgency was not something new, but rather a variant of an age-old form of irregular warfare designed to overwhelm conventional forces.

After teaching for a number of years Tanham joined the RAND Corporation, a think tank created by the Air Force to conduct sponsored research on defense and military affairs. His first book, *Communist Revolutionary Warfare: the Vietminh in Indochina*, appeared in 1961 and then was revised to include the early American experience in fighting the Viet Cong.

The communist strategy had its roots in China with Mao Tse-tung, but it was adapted to resist French attempts to regain control of Vietnam after World War II. Although Ho Chi Minh was the unchallenged leader of Vietnamese communist movement, the conflict was directed by his military commander, Vo Nguyen Giap. He modified Mao's thinking in a brilliant, flexible, and ruthless way to pursue his own brand of revolutionary warfare. Tanham described how the French army was bested at every turn and warned that a version of that same strategy was being used against the growing American military presence in Vietnam in the 1960s.

The doctrine of insurgent warfare was conducted in three distinct phases. The first, the strategic defensive, calls for a withdrawal in the face of superior conventional forces to stretch out enemy lines of communication and test its political will. The second or guerrilla phase is employed against an over-stretched enemy by irregular warfare to further weaken its resistance. During this phase irregular forces are organized into a conventional army. The third and final phase, the conventional or counteroffensive phase, is implemented as revolutionary forces gain military and moral superiority and set out to defeat an enemy on the battlefield.

But the Chinese model was tailored to the conflict in Vietnam. Tanham outlines Giap's planning to deploy a combination of regular and guerrilla forces to meet political and military objectives. However, both Mao and Giap recognized that the last phase of insurgency required proper timing to garner international support and be victorious on the ground. Giap mimicked the Chinese by creating different types of units: a regular army, regional forces, and popular or local troops. Each had parallel political organizations on every level of military command and emphasized troop indoctrination or political work in the army by party functionaries.

Giap was adept in managing the political-military implications of the war. For instance, he applied the western concept of security of the rear not only to lines of communication but to winning over the people to the revolutionary cause and ensuring his army had popular support. Conversely, he understood the enemy rear must be attacked —across the paddy fields and rural villages of the countryside to the provincial towns and cities of South Vietnam.

The communists also adhered to the primacy of the political in warfare. Unlike armies in the West, whose principal mission is fighting and winning wars, the Viet Minh had two missions, creating ideological uniformity throughout the country and developing an efficient modern army. Moreover, political training was regarded as important as military skills, and the army performed many tasks, from doing agricultural work to social mobilization at hamlet level.

Tanham recounts the futile attempts by the French to respond militarily and politically to the enemy, a strategy that was focused on pacifying the country-side by building political support. In response Giap fortified villages where his forces were strong and withdrew from others where his forces were weak—resorting to ambushes and the selected use of terror whenever the French made progress. But, according to Tanham, the French military proved less flexible and followed their established methods of fighting even when they were no longer effective.

Tanham analyzed the long siege of the French at Dien Bien Phu, the kind of combat that presaged the American experience in the second Indochina war. French casualties and prisoners in that defeat totaled 12,000 men—only six percent of French forces. However, the impact of that battle was political, not unlike the Tet offensive in 1968. But in both military and political terms, it signaled a critical turning point for the French armed forces and the beginning of their withdrawal from Indochina.

In addition to combining guerrilla and conventional forces on the battle-field, Giap also understood the tactical value of terror in achieving victory. When the South Vietnamese and American military sent medical cadres into the countryside to eliminate malaria, for example, they were brutally murdered by Viet Cong guerrillas. And later, when the South Vietnamese government attempted to spread democracy through the ballot box, the communists routinely assassinated political candidates. Moreover, Giap knew that international public opinion was key to victory, but he risked committing acts of terror against noncombatants—realizing that they would be condemned but not enough to off-set the political benefits of this tactic.

Terrorism and insurgency are related yet distinct types of irregular warfare. The former often is used by guerrillas and revolutionaries as a tactic which when properly targeted also can have an impact on the strategic level. Terrorism and insurgency also differ legally and morally. Terrorism is normally considered to be a criminal act whereas insurgency is covered under the Geneva Convention and has occurred in legitimate revolutionary movements throughout history. The French and American experiences in Indochina are important case studies in appreciating the operational distinctions between counterterrorism and counterinsurgency.

I met George Tanham in the 1980s while attending graduate school after my return from an advisory tour in El Salvador. In my attempt to understand U.S. strategy in Central America he encouraged me to study the lessons of past insurgencies. *Communist Revolutionary Warfare* remains a valuable primer on irregular warfare—as relevant today as when it was first published in the midst of the counterinsurgency era.

Michael A. Sheehan
June 2006

Ambassador Michael A. Sheehan served as Coordinator for Counterterrorism at the Department of State and, most recently, as Deputy Commissioner of Counter-Terrorism with the New York Police Department.

INDOCHINA BEFORE THE TRUCE OF 1954

PREFACE TO THE
REVISED EDITION

This book, originally written as a primer for those interested principally in the military aspects of the Vietminh struggle against the French during the years 1946-54, has now been updated to include three chapters on the Viet Cong. The first five chapters of the original version, now Part One of this revised edition, focus on the military apparatus of the Vietminh; no attempt has been made to present a narrative history or a description of all aspects of the Vietminh regime. However, even within this limited scope, the central theme of the Communist effort emerges: namely, the integration or orchestration of all means—political, economic, psychological, and military—to control the people and seize political power. Part One thus provides the basis for an under-standing of today's Viet Cong, who are in some cases the same people for-merly active in the Vietminh, plus new adherents strongly influenced by Vietminh doctrine and leadership.

In the new Part Two, Chapter VI traces the revival of insurgency in the South and the evolution of the Communist organization to include the National Liberation Front and the People's Revolutionary Party. Chapter VII deals with the basic Viet Cong military apparatus and analyzes the role of the National Liberation Army and the Viet Cong paramilitary forces, their organization, strategy, and tactics. Taking account of the massive U.S. participation which began in early 1965, Chapter VIII examines the impact of the American armed forces on the Viet Cong military, especially on the National Liberation Army and on the North Vietnamese regulars operating in the South.

As in the original edition, the emphasis here remains on the military aspects of the struggle. But it is clear that the same orchestration of effort applies to the Viet Cong and therefore few conclusions about the over-all course can be made from an examination of the military portion alone. Furthermore, the exact nature and direction of the conflict differ from place to place and time to time, and it is thus difficult to generalize about the Viet Cong military. The attempt is made, however, to distill the main characteristics of the Viet Cong. There is full recognition of the many exceptions to these generalizations and also of the fact that Viet Cong organization and tactics are constantly evolving—as is the strategy of the enemy and of the allies. But it is hoped that this brief summary will make a contribution to our understanding of the bitter struggle being waged in Vietnam today.

PREFACE TO THE FIRST EDITION

Recent events in Laos and South Vietnam indicate that the Communists are continuing their expansion in Southeast Asia. Although no formal invasions or declarations of war have been made, military actions ranging from ambushes to battalion-size engagements have taken place. Even more important, political indoctrination has been carried on extensively, with a consequent weakening of the authority of the legal governments. Although prediction of future events in this area must necessarily be uncertain, an examination of past Communist activities there should provide certain insights and thereby indicate means of coping with this continuing threat. This study focuses primarily on military aspects of the earlier war and attempts to provide insight by means of an analysis of Vietminh military doctrine, tactics, and organization as revealed during the earlier war in Indochina. Although no attempt has been made to present a narrative history or a description of all aspects of the Vietminh regime, the study clearly reveals the core of Communist revolutionary warfare, namely its emphasis on the integration of all means—political, economic, military, and psychological—to win the war, and, above all, to win the minds of the people.

The Vietminh success in Indochina clearly demonstrates the effectiveness of revolutionary warfare in an underdeveloped area. In both the strategic and tactical areas, it offered the Communists the greatest potential gain at the least possible risk. The initial low level of violence tended to preclude Western intervention, and at the same time involved the least risk of any possible loss of prestige for the Communists. It also enabled the Vietminh to pose as leaders of the insurgent nationalist movement and to gain popular support, while behind the scenes consolidating their power, which led to eventual control.

Tactically, guerrilla-type warfare enabled the Vietminh to retain mobility in the difficult jungle terrain, facilitated the gathering of intelligence information, and attrited the French forces, while permitting the Vietminh to build up the regular forces necessary for the formal battles of the final stage of the war. Thus, the major lesson to be learned by the West is that guerrilla operations of the Vietminh type will probably continue to be important, and that nuclear and other modern weapons have by no means rendered obsolete the more "primitive" forms of warfare.

Countries economically underdeveloped, and with strong feelings of resentment and dissatisfaction along with impatient aspirations, provide fertile ground for revolutionary movements. This combination of material needs and ideological poverty makes such countries particularly receptive to Communist aid and ideas.

If the free world is to prevail in the struggle against further Communist expansion and is to assist these countries in their own independent development, it must better understand their needs and the appeal and tactics of the Communists. It is hoped that this case study will assist in meeting the present challenge.

ACKNOWLEDGMENTS

It gives me pleasure to acknowledge the contribution of a number of individuals and organizations without whose help this book could not have been written.

Most of the research for Part One was done in Paris, where the French Army was most cooperative in giving me access to its war records and special studies on Indochina. I am indebted to General Cossé-Brissac, Director of the Service Historique de l'Armée; General Larroque, Director of the Centre d'Etudes Asiatiques et Africaines; and to many other French officers who must remain anonymous, for their valuable assistance and many courtesies.

My RAND colleagues—Victor M. Hunt, William W. Kaufmann, Edwin W. Paxson, Hans Speier, and Anne M. Jonas—deserve special thanks for their warm encouragement and valuable comments on the manuscript. And without the unstinting and expert editorial assistance of Sibylle Crane, this work might never have been completed.

I am deeply grateful to the United States Air Force and to The RAND Corporation for supplying the opportunity and the support that made this study possible, and for enabling me to visit Vietnam and thus gain first-hand knowledge of the physical conditions under which the war in Indochina was fought and of the people who fought it.

Part One of this book was written as a part of Project RAND, the research program conducted by The RAND Corporation for the U.S. Air Force. Needless to say, the opinions and conclusions expressed herein are entirely my own and do not reflect and official position of either the U.S. Air Force or The RAND Corporation.

Part Two was written as a personal effort and is based on my work and study in Vietnam since 1958, as well as on the reading of much of the vast literature on Vietnam. I had the opportunity to make trips to Vietnam in February and July, 1967, and to evaluate for myself the current situation there. I am indebted to a number of friends, mostly veterans of Vietnam, with whom I have had long and fruitful discussions about the Viet Cong and the war. I want to thank Gary Murfin, my research assistant, who helped in a variety of ways. Professor Joseph Zasloff and George Allen have read Part Two and made useful criticisms and suggestions. My secretary, Miss Lee Rademaker, on her own time has not only typed the manuscript but made helpful suggestions. As in the case of Part One, however, the opinions and views expressed are my own.

GEORGE K. TANHAM

INTRODUCTION

During World War II, an underground resistance movement—the Vietminh—developed in Indochina under the leadership of Ho Chi Minh. Although there can be little doubt today that this movement was largely Communist-inspired and that Ho himself was an old Communist, the spirit of nationalism was predominant at the time, and the revolutionary aspirations of the movement seemed confined to ousting the Japanese rulers. By the end of 1944, the Vietminh had set up a guerrilla high command. But, although supported and supplied by the United States, its relatively small force of poorly equipped guerrilla fighters was quite incapable of taking significant action against the Japanese.

In the spring and summer of 1945, the situation changed. On March 9, 1945, the Japanese disarmed and interned the French troops in Indochina, who until then had remained at liberty there in spite of the Japanese occupation. This act resulted in great loss of French prestige, particularly since it was becoming increasingly evident that the Japanese were losing the war. Thus the stage was set for release of all the forces for independence that had been gathering momentum over the years. Almost immediately the moderate Bao Dai, former Emperor of Annam, proclaimed himself "emperor" of an autonomous Vietnam. And two weeks later, General de Gaulle himself made some vague references to Vietnamese autonomy, hereby adding to nationalist hopes of gaining independence peacefully. Events shattered these hopes.

On August 10, the Vietminh High Command gave orders for a national uprising against the Japanese. Although officially directed only against Japan, the move was also obviously intended to forestall any subsequent return of the French. The revolt was so immediately successful in the north that Bao Dai abdicated his post of self-appointed titular head of the country. Ho Chi Minh formed a provisional government on August 29, and four days later proclaimed complete independence for Vietnam. With the success of this insurrection, the Communist element among Vietnamese nationalists gained a strong hold on the leadership of the revolutionary movement.

The French, although determined to reoccupy Vietnam, were for the moment stymied by their lack of troops and transportation. The Allies, however, came to their aid. In mid-September, British troops occupied the southern half of Indochina, and Chinese Nationalists the northern portion. The population's anti-British sentiment ran so high that the British commander, General Gracey, then found it necessary to proclaim martial law in his area. On September 23, a few French troops arrived at Saigon, seized the public buildings there, and immediately set about reestablishing French authority. Large French reinforcements arrived during October.

Ho Chi Minh realized that he faced a difficult situation and that if he were to succeed, it would be necessary to rally all Vietnamese nationalists to his cause. In an effort to disguise his Communist backing and in order to give his movement a patriotic stamp, he publicly dissolved the Communist Party on November 11 and formed a "national front." Actually, the Party went underground until 1951.

Before attempting the reconquest of the insurgent stronghold in the north, it was first necessary for the French to obtain the withdrawal of the Chinese Nationalists. In February, 1946, the French reached an agreement with Chiang Kai-shek that stipulated that Chinese troops would leave northern Vietnam, in return for which the French would give up all special rights in China. Ho appears to have been sufficiently impressed by this accord to decide that concessions to the French were necessary if he were to avoid the head-on collision for which he was as yet unprepared. At any rate, he agreed to French occupation of certain positions in north and central Vietnam. When French troops entered north Vietnam, they encountered both Chinese opposition and sporadic Vietminh attacks.

Efforts to arrive at a peaceful solution continued. On March 6, 1946, a *modus vivendi* was worked out whereby Ho allowed French troops to enter Haiphong and Hanoi, while France agreed to recognize Vietnam as a "free state." The French, perhaps deliberately, made no attempt to define this term precisely, a failure that later proved to be the germ of very serious difficulties. Neither side ever really accepted the March 6 agreement, and a series of conferences in the spring and summer of 1946 served merely to underline the irreconcilability of the two camps. The only tangible accords (such as the so-called "September agreement," which dealt chiefly with economic and cultural questions) tended to ignore the vital issues. While the French continued their military re-occupation, the Vietminh laid plans for the eventual ouster of all French troops.

On November 23, 1946, after a series of incidents in Haiphong, the French ordered the Vietnamese, under threat of reprisals, to evacuate their section of the city within two hours. Compliance with such an order was clearly impossible, and the French, true to the letter of their ultimatum, bombarded and wiped out the Vietnamese sections of Haiphong that same day.

This event, coupled with the patent inconclusiveness of the year's negotiations, apparently convinced the Vietminh of the hopelessness of this approach, and on December 19, the Vietminh ordered a surprise nationwide attack on all French forces. Though December 19 has become the commonly accepted date for the outbreak of the war, it is clear that intermittent hostilities between French and Vietnamese preceded this date by more than a year.

Throughout the war, Vietnamese independence remained the major political issue. In the earlier phase, the moderates in the nationalist camp were still open to a compromise with the French, under which they might have been ready to accept modified autonomy, had it been coupled with the promise of eventual independence. But the French, in their understandable unwillingness to surrender a prized possession and with shortsighted determination to avoid concessions in the direction of independence, remained blind to the possibility of an alliance against the Communist threat. French failure to support the moderate element thus vitiated an attempt by moderate nationalists, in May, 1947, to establish a "Front of National Union" in Saigon. By this and other evidence of their intransigence, the French slowly but inevitably alienated even the most conciliatory of the nationalists and drove most of them either into the revolutionary camp or into exile. In September, 1947, the French High Commissioner made a modest move in the right direction by offering "liberty within the French Union" to nationalist leaders, a proposal that was accepted by some of the moderates. Again, however, he failed to specify precisely what this phrase meant in practical terms. Moreover, the irate Vietminh took punitive action against those Vietnamese who had supported the proposal. Still, as late as 1948, the moderate Ngo Dinh Diem proposed to the French that they grant dominion status to Vietnam, a suggestion that was rejected.

In June, 1949, the French, perhaps in growing awareness of their error, invited Bao Dai to head a Vietnamese government, but by then most nationalists had become thoroughly distrustful of French motives, and the Communist Vietminh had clearly attained control over the nationalist movement. Bao Dai had neither popular support nor authority and showed little interest in governmental affairs.

To have underrated the force of nationalist feelings and to have disregarded all opportunities for genuine compromise may be called the basic French mistakes in Indochina. Failing to realize in time the crucial importance of popular support in this type of war, they remained oblivious to the fact that their disregard of popular will helped their enemy to consolidate forces and led thus to the inevitable success of the Vietminh.

Since 1950, when the U.S. Government began to provide aid to the French in their struggle against the Vietminh, the United States has become more and more involved in Indochina. The amount of aid, both military and economic, as well as the number of advisers has steadily increased. The United States refused to intervene to save the French from defeat at Dien Bien Phu; and although it was present as an observer, it did not participate as a member of the Geneva Conference in 1954. However, the U.S. Government provided material aid and moral support to Premier Diem and his new government in an effort to help build a viable regime in the South. It seemed for a few years that this attempt might succeed, but in the late 1950's, the regime began to flounder and the insurgency revived and grew stronger. Neither Diem nor the United States fully sensed or perceived the emerging danger until it became apparent in 1961. High-level missions from the United States in that year recommended stepped-up aid and more advisers. These were provided, but the situation continued to worsen. In November, 1963, Diem's regime was overthrown and a period of political instability began, with consequent military and political deterioration throughout the country. By 1964, there were more than 25,000 American advisers in South Vietnam, all but about 1,000 of whom were military, and the total aid amounted to about $1 billion per year. This effort to help the G.V.N. did not seem to slow the insurgency, which was aided and abetted from the North, and in early 1965 the United States felt compelled to begin bombing the North and to send troops to the South in order to save the situation. There are now nearly 500,000 ground troops in Vietnam, plus thousands of Air Force and Navy personnel in Vietnam and elsewhere in Southeast Asia supporting the effort. The cost is currently running about $25 billion and well over 50,000 American casualties a year. Still there appears to be no end in sight.

Chapter 1

VIETMINH MILITARY DOCTRINE AND THE WAR

In 1945, even before the Japanese surrender, Ho Chi Minh began to develop a regular army for the newly constituted Communist Vietminh government. The guerrillas of World War II (who had been trained and supplied mainly by the United States) were enrolled in this army and trained for conventional warfare. The Communist leadership believed that, given some time to build this kind of army, it could afford to wage war on the French, by then generally weakened, and drive them out of the country. Japanese and Allied armaments, though useful, were insufficient for the army's needs; it has been estimated that, in late 1946, Ho's force of 60,000 men had only 40,000 rifles. Nevertheless, on December 19, 1946, Ho suddenly launched attacks on the French forces in Hanoi and other garrison towns throughout the country. The inferiority of the Vietminh forces was very quickly revealed, and by spring 1947, the Vietminh government and the remnants of its army fled to the mountainous area north of Hanoi. A French operation in the fall of 1947 narrowly missed capturing Ho and destroying the remains of his army.

The inability of the Vietminh to achieve a quick victory, followed by the French failure to annihilate the Communist forces, indicated that a long war was likely. However, the Vietminh recognized this fact far more quickly and more clearly than the French. Consequently, the Vietminh leaders turned to the works of Mao Tse-tung for a theory of war. Their strategic concepts were to be strongly influenced by his ideas, which were singularly well suited to their own struggle. In *Strategic Problems of China's Revolutionary War,* Mao defined as basic to all revolutionary war the four main characteristics of the war in China: (1) a semicolonial country of great size and of uneven political and economic development; (2) the presence of a powerful enemy; (3) a Red Army that started out by being weak as well as small; and (4) a Communist leadership that could rely on popular acceptance of the revolutionary idea, at least in the sense of an agrarian revolution. Whereas factors 2 and 3 pointed to a long war and, Mao warned, might even spell defeat if there were bungling by the revolutionary leadership, factors 1 and 4 strongly favored ultimate success. Starting with these assumptions, which today may appear rather obvious premises, Mao went on to develop his theory of a protracted war in three stages, culminating in victory for the revolution.

In his *On Protracted War,* Mao again started with the specific case of China. While rejecting the idea that China could be subjugated by counterrevolutionary forces, he warned that it would be equally false to believe in a quick and easy victory for the revolution. The war will be long, and will be divisible into three definite stages, whose length cannot be predicted. In the first, given the initial military superiority of the enemy, the revolutionary forces must be on the strategic defensive, while the enemy holds the strategic initiative. During this phase, the Communists must be willing, if necessary, to trade territory, industries, and population for the preservation of their weak military forces. They must be prepared for long retreats, during which they may temporarily grow even weaker. The enemy, however, will also be growing weaker because of lengthening logistic lines, harassment by the Red guerrillas, weakening morale, and increasing unfriendliness of the population. The next stage will begin when the enemy stops his advance and concentrates on holding territory and consolidating his gains. During this second period, as in the first, guerrilla action will be the chief form of warfare, while the regular revolutionary forces are being trained and equipped for the final stage of the war—the counteroffensive, the objective of which will be to annihilate the enemy. In the course of the second phase, the revolutionary forces, though perhaps strategically inferior to the enemy, must gain the tactical numerical superiority that will enable them to win battles. The crucial timing of the counteroffensive will depend not only on the internal situation of the two warring sides but on the international situation as well.

Mao's concept of the protracted war in three stages served as the theoretical basis for the revolutionary war in Indochina. The scope of the present study precludes a detailed comparison of China in 1936 with Indochina after World War II, but it may be helpful to examine the extent to which Mao's four main characteristics of the Chinese situation applied to Indochina.

About one-thirteenth the size of China, Indochina has about one-twentieth its population. Outside the two populous delta regions, there are large, sparsely populated areas which afford shelter for irregular forces and create difficulties for a modern army. A colonial country, unevenly developed both politically and economically, Indochina was initially unable to put into the field a modem army that could stand up to the strong French forces stationed on its soil. Thus, Indochina, like China, provided the opportunity for a strategic defensive and the evolution of the protracted war. However, the Vietminh demonstrated that guerrillas could operate not only in the mountains and thinly populated areas but also in the heavily populated enemy regions, and, indeed, that to some extent it was possible clandestinely to develop a military machine in such areas. While recognizing major dissimilarities between the two countries and certain factors specific to each, one can see the struggle in both wars primarily as one between an underdeveloped regime with limited arms and resources against a more modern power backed by highly developed military forces, though in the case of Indochina the French were 8,000 miles away from their industrial base. However, it is also clear that the Chinese struggle took the form of a civil war among the Chinese, while in Vietnam the war was waged against a foreign power.

Little seems to be known of what Viet leaders were thinking during 1948. The available information indicates that they had accepted the theory of the protracted war and resigned themselves to the fact that they were in the harsh first phase. They confined themselves chiefly to guerrilla warfare throughout the country. Attacks by regular units the following year showed, however, that they had secretly been building regular forces.

VO NGUYEN GIAP AND THE FORMULATION
OF VIET DOCTRINE

For 1949, reports of meetings and speeches by Vietminh leaders permit us to form a more precise idea of the emerging strategy. At a military congress in mid-May, top military leaders expounded the doctrine of the protracted war and stated at which stage they considered the war in Indochina to be. According to Colonel Ly Ban, an officer in the Ministry of National Defense, the military mission of the revolutionary forces would be accomplished in three phases: passive resistance, active resistance and preparation for the counteroffensive, and, finally, the general counteroffensive. Hoang Van Thai, Chief of the General Staff, echoed the same idea. Speaking particularly of the passing from the second to the final phase, he stated his belief that partial offensives should precede the general counteroffensive, and that, before launching the latter, the Vietminh would have to have a tactical force far superior to that of the enemy. Vo Nguyen Giap, Commander in Chief of the Vietminh army, stressed the need to consolidate the principal revolutionary forces. Praising the troops but criticizing the quality of higher officers, he called for improvement in the cadres and the commands and for fullest development of popular support for the regular army. The struggle, he said, was in the second stage, where guerrilla warfare was most important and the war of movement of secondary value. Yet he thought that there ought to be progressively more and larger offensive actions in preparation for the general counteroffensive, and insisted that, before one could afford to pass into the final stage, the war of movement would have to become equal in importance to guerrilla action.

As Colonel Ly Ban pointed out, World War II had shown that guerrillas alone could not win wars, and therefore a war of movement became a necessity. The war of movement, as Vietminh leaders conceived it, was characterized chiefly by the absence of fixed fronts and rear areas, quick concentration for action, and immediate disengagement after fighting. In a seeming paradox, although the Vietminh always spoke of a war of movement and of the importance of avoiding pitched battles, the war was essentially one of attrition, in the sense that all efforts, military and nonmilitary, were aimed at wearing down the French. This was particularly true of the first two phases of the war, when the enemy was being weakened for the *coup de grâce* of the third stage. But an essential part of this overall strategy of attrition was the multitude of tactical operations, as well as the decisive offensive of the third phase, all of which were based on movement and mobility.

The outstanding military figure of the Vietminh was Vo Nguyen Giap. Born in 1912, he became a Communist at an early age and was a veteran of French jails before World War II. His anti-French feelings were further intensified when the French police, he claimed, killed his wife and sister-in-law. Giap studied revolutionary tactics in China, gained experience in organizing guerrillas in World War II, and became head of the Vietminh guerrilla command in 1944. A former history teacher and holder of an advanced degree, he urged his troops to study and reflect on their own combat experiences so as to improve themselves continuously.

Moreover, Giap took his own advice, and the fruit of his reflections and self-critique was a book, published in 1950, entitled *La guerre de la libération et l'armée populaire (The War of Liberation and the Popular Army),* which still remains one of the fullest expressions of Vietminh doctrine. While accepting Mao's concept of a three-phase war, Giap felt uncertain about the possibility of drawing clear divisions between the several stages. This uncertainty may have arisen from his awareness of the unique situation of Indochina, with her two major theaters of operations—the southern area around the Mekong Delta and the northern one around the Red River (or Tonkin) Delta. Progress in the two areas had been quite different and was to continue so to the end of the war. In the north, the Vietminh in 1945–46 built up a regular army, which took the field against the French but was quickly defeated. Nothing like this happened in the south. By the end of the war, the north was entering phase three, while the south had hardly emerged from phase one. Only in the northern theater of operations, therefore, can the development of the three phases be traced fairly clearly.

Giap claimed that the failure of the French to defeat the Vietminh in the north in 1946–47 had marked the end of any hope for a short war and, he implied, had allowed the factors determining a protracted war to come into play.

To understand Giap's critique of Vietminh strategy, one must recall the developments of the early war period. During the first phase of the revolution, which began in the south (Cochinchina and South Annam) in 1945, the Vietminh took the strategic defensive. In the north, on the other hand, various agreements with the French accorded Ho's government *de facto* recognition, and the uneasy peace lasted until the surprise Vietminh attack of December, 1946. By these agreements, the Vietminh gained time in which to prepare their military forces and to win popular support. In their propaganda campaign, they could point to these accords as indications of their own love of peace, and when it became expedient to break them, they argued that it was in fact the French who had broken them and so precipitated the war. The failure of the attacks of 1946–47 forced the Viets into the defensive in the north also and ushered in the first phase of the protracted war. After the regular forces had been beaten and their remnants compelled to disguise themselves as civilians or to seek shelter in the area northwest of Hanoi, the war continued clandestinely. While the Viets were sacrificing—carefully, however—territory, people, and economic assets in order to preserve a hard core, they never relaxed their efforts to win over the population. The activities of clandestine cells, guerrillas, and propaganda agents proved increasingly damaging to the French, and slowly the Vietminh gained the loyalty of many of the people. Ho and Giap clearly had accepted Mao's precepts regarding the importance of preserving the cadres and winning popular support.

Although Giap never mentions the disastrous attacks of December, 1946, in his book, he obviously found profitable lessons in the Viet failures of this early period. In the first place, he saw that a sound strategy alone was not enough; good tactics also were a necessity. Among the tactical mistakes, he included poorly conceived ambushes, efforts to hold certain terrain too long, and attempts at encirclement after the enemy had received strong reinforcements. In this connection, Giap noted the dangers conventional warfare held for weak forces: "For an army relatively feeble and poorly equipped, the classical concept of war is extremely dangerous and ought to be resolutely rejected." He pointed out that the greatest failures had come about when the Vietminh had departed from guerrilla tactics and attempted formal battles. Failure in the south, he believed, was due to inadequate political guidance for the troops and ineffective training, while in the north it was attributable more to improper military training and insufficient understanding of the true nature of guerrilla warfare. Lastly, Giap thought that it had been a strategic mistake not to regard Indochina as a single theater and, consequently, that the neglect of Cambodia and Laos had been a basic error in the conduct of the war. (In this respect, the writer believes that Giap was mistaken: Geographically, racially, and historically, Indochina was not homogeneous, and the subsequent attempts to make it into one strategic area failed.)

According to Giap, the second phase of the war had begun in 1947, and at the time of his writing (in 1950) was still in effect.[1] The intervening years had been favorable to the Vietminh, both in their own revolutionary achievements and in the developments that were taking place in the French camp. The Vietminh had continued their strategy of defense and had built up the size and quality of their forces. He wrote:

> The activities of the independent companies conducted at the same time as those of the armed propaganda teams, the guerrilla units, and the village militia were the principal forms of combat used to advance our guerrilla war, to destroy enemy reserves, and to protect our own reserves. Since popular "bases" were indispensable to the development of the guerrilla war, we dispersed the companies of each battalion and we permitted them the necessary liberty of action so that they could infiltrate different regions and cement their friendly relations with the local populace. Since the companies were relatively weak, they had no difficulty in understanding the necessity for firm popular bases. Thanks to their intimate acquaintance with the different regions, they easily won the support of the local population. Their close connection with popular bases gave a strong impetus to the armed conflict. When the guerrilla units acquired enough experience, when the local militia became powerful enough, the dispersed elements of the companies in the different localities gradually regrouped themselves.

The winter of 1949–50, in particular, was described by Giap as a period of visible progress for the Vietminh. The rate of preparation increased, offensive actions became more frequent and daring, and small units were developing into larger line units. There was increased emphasis on the regular forces and the war of movement. The regional and communal forces, however, were not neglected, and guerrilla warfare was, if anything, intensified.[2] He summarized the effort as follows: "We must work without stopping to improve the conditions of our forces, to attrite the enemy forces, to make the balance gradually tip in our favor in order to proceed rapidly toward the third phase."

Giap believed that the French at this time had turned primarily to defensive warfare and had reduced their goals in Indochina. To some extent this was true. Although the French continued to carry out clearing operations and limited offensives in the late forties, they never again came so close to complete victory as they had been in 1947. They had considerable success with pacification efforts in the south, and the Vietminh leaders admitted this fact. However, Giap clearly recognized the weaknesses of the French situation. He predicted that, as the war wore on, the French would have to use colonial troops and even Vietnamese,[3] that they would never have adequate manpower or supplies, and that their morale would decline.

Both Giap and Ho Chi Minh regarded 1950 as the decisive year, and intimated that phase three was not far off. According to Giap, the three requirements for passage to the third phase were superiority of the revolutionary forces, a favorable world situation, and a noticeable weakening of the enemy. He wrote: "We will not move into a general counteroffensive until our strength in all areas [political, economic, and military] is reflected in our military strength." In 1950, the

Vietminh army was approaching in number that of the French and was developing the capability to concentrate and maneuver in major campaigns. Many French troops were increasingly tied to forts and bases, permitting the Vietminh to attain tactical superiority more easily. The arrival of Chinese forces at the border, in December, 1949, presaged outside aid. The military capability of the French, on the other hand, was suffering increasingly from lack of reinforcements, from dispersion, and from logistic difficulties; the French clearly were on the defensive, and their will to fight was weakening. Perhaps most important, French procrastination over Vietnamese independence had alienated more and more of the population.

Giap's optimism in 1950, however, was still qualified by several reservations. For one thing, he considered the French military forces still superior to his own battle corps because they possessed a more effective command system, more and better equipment, and greater firepower. Furthermore, he confessed that the execution of the war of movement, which alone could bring victory, had proved more complicated than he had foreseen. A shortage of staff officers and specialists made the solution of command, communications, and logistic problems unexpectedly difficult. Lastly, and quite significantly, he indirectly admitted that there were still large segments of the population that had not been won over to the Vietminh cause and hence would not provide a secure base for regular-army operations.[4]

Giap's view of phase three, which he described as the stage of "the general counteroffensive," whose primary objectives were to annihilate the enemy and reconquer the national territory, was not as simple as Mao's. The name was given not because it implied an attack on all fronts, but because it led to final victory. He conceived of this phase as having several subdivisions, only in the last of which would there be formal battles. Before progressing to the third phase, the Vietminh would have to be certain of (1) the absolute moral superiority of the revolutionary forces; (2) a considerable improvement in the material position of their army that would narrow the French economic advantage (Giap described the agricultural economy of Indochina as ideal for guerrilla actions but less so for larger, more formal operations); (3) an international situation more and more favorable to the Communists; and (4) a strong and purposeful direction of the war by the Communist leadership, in contrast to less and less sure command by the enemy. In all four respects, he thought, the Vietminh would benefit greatly by the widening disagreements between the French and the Americans and by the political divisions within France.

All forms of warfare were to be employed during stage three, but the war of movement would become more and more important, while guerrilla warfare would assume secondary value. There would also be an increasing number of formal engagements. The war of movement, in Giap's opinion, was best suited to the Communist forces, for it not only took advantage of their superior morale but allowed them to corner and annihilate the enemy. Guerrilla warfare, however, would always remain important because it, too, depended on high morale and, moreover, was less handicapped by inferiority in matériel. Furthermore, in the final phase, the irregular forces would be a major link in the logistic system of the regular army.

Giap contended that the final phase might be long or short and that its duration could not be entirely controlled by the Vietminh, though they could influence it. The absolute moral superiority of the Vietminh might make the phase short because:

> This will enable us to accelerate our pace, aided by the willing sacrifice of the population, their resistance and revolt in regions occupied by the enemy, and because of the increase in our forces due to general mobilization and help from abroad. This superiority could bring about great reverses to the enemy: dislocation of rebel troops, growth of antiwar sentiment among French troops. The French domestic situation could be severely affected by defeats in Indochina, by pacifism, and by independence movements in the colonies. Grave errors might be made by the French in their strategy.

On the other hand, the material poverty of the Vietminh, continued French resistance in the south, and more active American and British intervention could prolong the phase. If this were the case, the war would take on the more classic form of warfare, with pitched battles and long campaigns.

THE USE OF MAO'S THEORY

Mao's theory of the protracted war provided an outline for the conduct of the revolutionary war in Indochina, and several principles of his were stressed in Vietminh doctrine. One of these was the "security of the rear." This term did not mean to the Vietminh what it does to Western military persons. In Western terminology, it is a way of saying that provisions have been made by the military forces to assure the functioning of the rear echelons without enemy interference. To the Vietminh, "security of the rear" meant that the people of the country had been won over to the revolutionary cause and that wherever the army operated, it would receive warm support. The army depended on the population to form a secure base for its operations. Once the people had been indoctrinated, it was not enough for them merely to be sympathetic to the cause. The regular army relied on them for such positive contributions as food, shelter, intelligence, and transport. When necessary, the local inhabitants also provided hiding places for the troops, and often accepted them into their midst for long periods of time.

Popular support alone, however, did not govern the choice of areas of operation. There are indications that such other circumstances as terrain and enemy initiative, and especially the combination of these two factors, may have been even stronger determinants. Because of French concentration in the Red River Delta, the Vietminh were forced to remain and operate chiefly in the mountainous areas outside the Delta, where the various minorities were not particularly sympathetic. These people believed the Vietminh to be a Vietnamese movement, and as they had always disliked the Vietnamese, they now distrusted the Vietminh. The Vietnamese, on the other hand, who were the most sympathetic to the Vietminh cause, lived in the Delta and coastal regions, where the Vietminh could not operate freely.

The principle of the security of the rear—in reverse, as it were—governed the Vietminh's efforts to create insecurity in enemy-held areas. To this end, guerrilla groups were organized in the French areas, which very effectively not only harassed the French military forces, but politically indoctrinated the population and undermined the French regime and, later, the French-sponsored national Vietnamese government. These Communist cells waged propaganda war and established shadow governments in the villages and sometimes even in larger administrative units. Certain Vietminh adherents (known as *Dich Van*) even attached themselves to the French forces in order to defect as soon as their leaders ordered them to do so.

The importance of the guerrilla fighter in the Vietminh theory of war can hardly be exaggerated. Active in all phases of the war, he was effective in constructive as well as destructive ways. Whereas the Soviets had considered the guerrilla a useful auxiliary to the Red Army, the Vietminh used him in many more ways and proved that he could operate anywhere. Aside from their obvious tasks of sabotaging, harassing, ambushing, and attacking the enemy, the Viet guerrillas waged political warfare in both friendly and enemy areas. Often they provided some of the screening and security forces for the regular army; they also "prepared the battlefield" (which involved stockpiling, intelligence-gathering, and sometimes fortification), and fought against the French clearing operations. On many occasions, they were called upon for logistic help. The Vietminh experience showed, furthermore, that guerrillas could be developed even in urban areas, as, for example, in the French-held outskirts of Saigon. As will be shown later, Giap also infiltrated regular units into the thickly populated Tonkin Delta, where they acted as guerrillas.

Again following the Chinese lead, the Vietminh formed "bases" that served several purposes. In Viet definition, the characteristics of a base area are "a closely integrated complex of villages prepared for defense; a politically indoctrinated population in which even children have their specific intelligence tasks; a network of food and weapons dumps; an administrative machine parallel to that of the legal authority, to which may be added at will any regular [army] unit assigned to operations in the area." The typical base thus was equipped to serve as a nucleus for Vietminh government and a strongpoint for military operations. These organizations might be clandestine or open, depending on the situation. The most important of the early base areas was northwest of Hanoi.

Mao had recognized the difficulty of selecting the right moment for launching the general counteroffensive, and the Chinese had had considerable arguments over this question of timing. The Vietminh experienced similar difficulties and differences of opinion. Giap, while fully accepting Mao's doctrine of the protracted war, seemed impatient to pass into phase three. Although his own analysis of the situation in 1950 had revealed his reservations about the Vietminh capability at that time, he pressed for going into the offensive during the first months of that year. He was opposed by the head of the Communist Party, who argued that conditions were not yet favorable for phase three. Just how widely this issue was discussed is not known, but the military congress of 1950 approved Giap's plans.

During the last half of 1949, the French had shifted their primary field of operations from Cochinchina in the south to Tonkin in the north. The most important reason for this move was the arrival of Chinese Communist forces at the Indochina border. Furthermore, the French were concerned over the growing strength of the Vietminh in the north, and felt that the success of pacification in the south rendered this transfer of the main effort possible and safe. There were dangers involved, however, as the shift of large numbers of troops to the northern area detracted from the clearing operations and the maintenance of the *status quo* in the south.

The north having become the most important theater of operations, Giap struck at the string of French forts on the Chinese frontier in the autumn of 1950, and, in the famous battle of Route Coloniale 4, nearly annihilated the French garrisons. Giap himself appeared surprised by the extent of his victory and was slow to follow up his success. According to many observers, Giap's forces, despite this successful action, were not ready for open battle because the regular army was not yet fully formed. This contention seems to be borne out by the subsequent limited defeats inflicted on Giap by French forces under Marshal de Lattre at Vinh Yen (January, 1951) and Mao Khé (March, 1951), and by the partial defeat at the Day River (May, 1951). After these reverses, Giap withdrew his forces at the end of the fighting season and set about recruiting, equipping, and training a stronger army.

Marshal de Lattre, who took command in Indochina in December, 1950, not only followed but improved on the tactics of his predecessor, General Carpentier. Carpentier had established a system of posts and forts to protect the Tonkin Delta and to provide a secure base, relying on mobile units for offensive operations. The marshal regrouped his troops and organized mobile groups to act as his striking forces and to provide mobile reserves. These measures required a great number of men, and consequently some outposts were relinquished and certain areas voluntarily surrendered to the Vietminh. But, whereas De Lattre apparently had been trying to create a secure base from which to strike out offensively, his successors, after his death early in 1952, became more and more tied to the defensive functions of this system. Also, De Lattre had been singularly able to inspire his troops; succeeding commanders, on the other hand, were increasingly faced with morale problems.

In November, 1951, the French struck at and captured Hoa Binh, thereby severing the north-south communications route of the Vietminh. Giap counterattacked, but the French had anticipated his move and indeed had planned to attrite his forces in a set battle. Giap suffered heavy casualties but continued the battle for three months, engaging in a protracted campaign of position warfare that was contrary to Mao's ideas.[5] Faced with increasing supply problems, heavy losses, and Vietminh infiltration of the Delta, the French reluctantly abandoned Hoa Binh. They deprecated the seriousness of this withdrawal by claiming that they had by then accomplished their objective of forcing Giap into pitched battles, with resulting heavy casualties.

THE TIME OF SELF-APPRAISAL

In August, 1952, at the seventh anniversary celebration of the Vietminh revolution that had led to the establishment of the People's Republic, the Vietminh leaders admitted some of their mistakes in the intervening years; clearly aware of the setbacks of 1951, they forecast a long war. As Vice President Pham Van Dong put it, "Resistance is in the seventh year of its existence. It still will last a long time and many difficulties remain to be surmounted." Truong Chinh stressed the need for guerrilla activity, and even Giap said that the Vietminh "must energetically pursue the fight in the enemy's rear." All the speakers agreed on the need to wear down the French still further and to conquer the rural masses politically. The tenor of the speeches was far more guarded and less optimistic than had been the case in 1949–50; it was evident that the Vietminh had underestimated the enemy and miscalculated the timing of the counteroffensive (though Ho still spoke of it as "coming in the near future").

Even during this period of rebuilding and self-examination, however, Giap apparently felt compelled to continue the offensive. Possibly, he believed the situation to be ripe and attributed his earlier failures to improper tactics. But it is equally possible that he had a correct estimate of the situation but found more compelling reasons for staying on the offensive, which, in view of the 1951 defeats, meant abandoning the precepts of Mao. Although we cannot be sure what his motivations were, scattered evidence points to the important conclusion that, for once, there were serious morale problems in the Vietminh camp in general and in the army in particular. Success in the autumn of 1950 may have raised hopes that made the defeats of the following spring all the more disappointing. Some peasant unrest had been created by the Vietminh land reforms and changed fiscal policies. According to the French, Ho had never really captured the peasant support in the way Mao had in China, and his supporters among the peasants were adventurers and malcontents. While the French charge is obviously exaggerated, there is little doubt that Viet leaders had some problems of morale in the army and among the peasantry at this time.

Giap now reverted to operational tactics that avoided pitched battles and attempted instead to draw the French out of their strong points in the Delta. This strategy of *zones excentriques,* as the French called it, was rather similar to Liddell Hart's "indirect approach." Giap decided to strike in areas that, although lightly held, had certain political and psychological value to the French and called for at least a token defense. The obvious choice for such operations were those mountain areas where certain ethnic minorities had remained sympathetic to the French. The invasion of the Thai[6] country, in September, 1952, was an excellent example of this strategy, and it worked exactly as Giap had planned it. Except for the single tactical mistake of staging a prolonged attack on one of the French strongholds, the operation was brought off expertly.

As the French forces were concentrated in the Red River Delta, the mountainous regions were weakly held, but for obvious reasons the French were reluctant to evacuate them. They were thus faced with the dilemma of having either to abandon these mountain people or to dispatch forces from the Delta, thereby weakening the Delta defenses. Even if they chose the latter alternative, they could not afford to send out forces adequate to cope with Giap's main force in these difficult areas, for to do so would have been to leave the Delta open to massive infiltration. In the end, the French avoided making what may indeed have been an impossible choice, and tried, instead, to follow both courses. As a result, they were unable to muster sufficient strength in either area; the forces they sent into the mountains proved inadequate there, but their absence seriously weakened the Delta defenses. The defeat at Dien Bien Phu was in large part the result of a similar error in French strategy.

In the autumn of 1953, the French concluded a treaty with Laos that provided for membership of this mountain kingdom in the French Union under conditions very satisfactory to the French. The possibility of a Vietminh invasion of Laos, however, aroused French concern, and, in November, General Navarre decided to occupy Dien Bien Phu in order to force Giap to cope with this strong-hold before invading Laos. Navarre also hoped to create such a strong camp that the Viet attack would be not only unsuccessful but costly. Thus, the occupation of Dien Bien Phu was to serve the dual purpose of protecting Laos and forcing the Viets to attack a strongly held position to their own detriment.

The announcement, in January, that an Allied conference was to convene at Geneva the following April to deal with the problem of Indochina apparently influenced the Vietminh to make an all-out effort against Dien Bien Phu— even to the point of accepting a siegelike battle and heavy casualties—for the sake of political gains at Geneva. Giap now recalled the 308th Division, which was even then engaged in the invasion of Laos that the French had meant to forestall, and put it around Dien Bien Phu.

April 26 marked the opening of the Geneva Conference and the beginning of the final, bloody assault on Dien Bien Phu. Slowly but surely, Vietminh superiority of numbers and firepower ground down the French position. On May 8, the garrison surrendered, and the Vietminh had won a tremendous political victory.

This battle, while violating one of the major tenets of Viet doctrine (namely, that pitched battles, and particularly sieges, must be avoided), confirmed certain others. First and foremost, it demonstrated the importance of subordinating military considerations to political ends. Though the battle of Dien Bien Phu clearly hurt Giap's battle corps (the French estimated that his losses doubled theirs), the political advantages and the blow to French morale in Indochina, and particularly in France, far outweighed these losses. The experience of Dien Bien Phu also revealed the virtue of the Vietminh's painstaking preparation for battle, their skill and diligence in camouflage and digging in. It is hard to determine whether the use of direct artillery fire, which may have been decisive, was forced on the Viets by their crews' lack of training in the conventional use of artillery, or whether it was deliberately chosen as most appropriate for the terrain.

In a strictly military sense, the defeat at Dien Bien Phu was not necessarily catastrophic for the French. Giap had suffered heavily. Furthermore, the French garrison, while important enough, accounted for only one-fifteenth of the total number of French troops in Indochina. But the political repercussions, as foreseen by the Viet leaders, were such that Paris decided to end the struggle.

NOTES

1. Most observers would place the beginning of phase two in 1949, as the French retained the initiative during 1947–49 and the first Vietminh attacks of a formal nature did not occur until 1949.

2. For a more detailed discussion of the distinguishing characteristics of the regular army, the regional troops, and the popular forces, and of their relationship to one another, see pp. 19–22.

3. It should be remembered that French law prohibited the use of French conscripts outside France; hence the full burden of the war fell on the French regular army and the Foreign Legion.

4. It is true that more and more of the people were alienated by the French, but they did not therefore all rally enthusiastically to the Vietminh cause. Even those, however, who merely became indifferent thereby created difficulties for the French and thus indirectly aided the Vietminh.

5. The French, by striking at one of the enemy's more weakly held key points, may have taught Giap a trick he was later to use against them.

6. Part of Indochina, not Thailand.

Chapter 2

THE VIETMINH MILITARY ORGANIZATION

The twofold objective of the Vietminh military organization was to create ideological uniformity throughout the country and to develop an efficient modern army. To these ends, the Communist leadership set out to develop a military machine with strict political controls, centralized authority, and uniform territorial organization. Almost from the beginning, the military forces were divided into three groups of varying combat capabilities: the regular army, the regional forces, and the popular troops. Furthermore, the Communist Party maintained a political organization within the army that paralleled the military at all echelons. These were the few basic organizational characteristics that remained unchanged throughout the war. For the rest, the Vietminh's dedication to the Communist principle that organization should not be static but should reflect progress, and their acceptance of Mao's theory of the protracted war in three stages, meant that the military establishment had to be in a constant state of organizational evolution. The need for practical experimentation under atypical war conditions further contributed to this state of flux. In the course of time, small guerrilla groups grew into modern divisions, which in turn underwent modifications. The simple guerrilla command of 1944, after numerous changes, became the complex general staff of 1954. The political organization within the army, cautious and limited in its powers of control during the first years of struggle, ultimately developed into a highly influential organism.

In the last years of the war, the National Military Council, composed of President Ho and the ministers of Defense, Interior, and Finance, directed the overall war effort. Responsibility for the military conduct of the war lay with the Ministry of National Defense, whose internal organization, too, was altered as old problems were solved and new ones arose.

Early in the war, the Vietminh shared high government positions with leaders of nationalist groups. But gradually, as they perfected their Party organization, developed Communist leaders at the lower echelons, and gained greater popular support, they began to ease non-Communists out of responsible positions. Certainly, by the early 1950's, the Viets had won a tight hold on the military apparatus and were pursuing Communist ends in addition to their nationalist objectives.[1]

At the time of the cease-fire, the Ministry of National Defense was headed by Vo Nguyen Giap. As Commander in Chief of the army, Giap had operational control as well as administrative responsibilities. The ministry was organized on the Chinese pattern, with three major subdivisions: the Political Bureau, the General Directorate of Supplies and Maintenance, and the General Staff.

THE POLITICAL BUREAU

The Vietminh regime, like any other Communist government, attached enormous importance to the political aspects of war. A political organization within the military establishment was designed to assure proper ideological indoctrination of the soldiers and the integration of military actions with political objectives. In the early years of the war, when co-operation with national groups was policy, the power of the political agents (commissars) was still limited; military commanders had the final decision on military issues, while the activities of the political officers were restricted to purely political matters. As the Vietminh element in the government became more powerful, however, the balance shifted. By 1950, there were specific instructions stating that, in case of a conflict between the military commander and the political commissar, the latter's view was decisive. (The Russian experience, however, may lead one to overestimate the role of the commissars. In Indochina, as in China, most military leaders were themselves Communists, who had fought long and hard for the movement, were generally loyal to its goals, and thus required relatively little political supervision.)

By the end of the war, the Political Bureau had been established within the Ministry of Defense as the highest organ for political control in the armed forces. Both the territorial commands and the divisions had what were called "Delegated Political Commissars." Even in temporary commands, such as the "fronts,"[2] political officers maintained close supervision over all activities. In the higher units, these men would be assisted by various committees. At the division level, for instance, there were committees for administration, political instruction, recreation, preparation of the battlefield, propaganda for civilians, propaganda against the enemy, and the affairs of the Party. At lower levels, the organization became simpler. No political commissars existed below the company level, but in every platoon a political cell worked closely with the company political officer. At company level, there was a political organization called the Military Council, composed of men who were elected by the members of the company for a three-month term but were subject to recall. This council was a "democratic" device, whose alleged purpose was "to educate the troops and provide political guidance, not to allow the men to argue or dispute with the officers." When the company was divided, the various platoons had their individual, smaller military councils.

Parallel to the official political organization within the army, there apparently was a clandestine Party organization, which at certain levels merged with the political organization. Every company and battalion had its Communist cell, with a subcell for each company section, and a secretary who was responsible for the work and discipline of both cell and subcell. If the cell had more than nine members, it elected a smaller group, called the Committee of Delegates, to work with the secretary as an executive committee. At regimental and at division level, the Party organization merged with the political organization in the Subcommittee for Party Affairs under the political commissar.

While Party organization men, by definition, were members of the Communist Party, this was usually, but not necessarily, true of officials in the political organization. The political officers wore uniforms and were members of the armed forces, but they enjoyed a privileged position.

THE GENERAL DIRECTORATE OF SUPPLIES AND MAINTENANCE

The second major subdivision of the Defense Ministry, the General Directorate of Supplies and Maintenance, had four bureaus: food, clothing, and equipment; armament and ammunition; health; and transport. These services were nowhere as complex as their modern Western equivalents. Before the emergence of the regular army, the supply system was largely decentralized; only with formation of the battle corps and the advent of massive Chinese aid did it become more centralized and complex. Little is known about its organization, but the operation of the logistic system will be discussed more fully in the chapter following.

THE HIGH COMMAND AND GENERAL STAFF

The Vietminh High Command, from its inception, had a wide variety of responsibilities, some of them not normally those of a high command. In the beginning, one of its major functions was that of guerrilla command. (Although there was a so-called General Staff, it was very rudimentary in form.) In April, 1947, the Supreme Command, as it was then called, had five major subdivisions: an Intelligence Service, a Political Service, a Bureau for Popular Troops, an Inspector General, and a General Staff. The General Staff was very simple in its organization and was concerned with operations, which at that time consisted mainly of small but numerous guerrilla actions. Its other major function, in the early stage of the war, was the training and organization of larger units, with the ultimate objective of forming a modern field army. Operations and training remained the General Staff's primary missions until late 1949 or early 1950, when planning, in the Western sense of the word, began to play a much larger role in the work of the High Command.

In 1950, a more modern General Staff, based largely on the French model, was created or, more precisely, reorganized from the older one. The cabinet of this new General Staff had four sections: local security, communications, accounts, and administration. The four major staff officers were in charge of personnel, intelligence, operations, and supply, much as is the case in the American army. Under the General Staff were the territorial commands and the line outfits (then regiments). The organizational pattern made it apparent that the staff was intended to plan and direct the operations of large units. Its strongest point was probably intelligence, its weakest, supply. Also, Giap lacked sufficient numbers of trained staff officers, and many of the weaknesses of his organization were a reflection of this shortage.

THE GENERAL STAFF AFTER 1953

By 1953, the staff organization had become still more elaborate, and the changes clearly reflected Chinese influence. The four familiar staff divisions had been dropped and replaced by the more numerous Chinese "bureaus." Vietminh officers were being trained in Chinese schools, and a large group of Chinese advisers was attached to the Viet army, especially to the General Staff. The latter now had ten bureaus, in keeping with its growth and the widening scope of its activities. The two most important were the Political Bureau of the Staff, listed first on the organizational charts, and the Directorate of Operations. Working closely with these two, but organizationally under them, was the Bureau of Important Affairs, in charge of training and planning for at least six months ahead.

As the Vietminh developed divisions and began to anticipate operations of larger scope, they had to plan much further ahead, not only for the usual military reasons, but because of several factors peculiar to the situation in Indochina. One of these was the phenomenon of the "front," temporary headquarters specially established for individual operations involving units of the battle corps. Every front required a certain amount of time to make its plans and to become operational. These fronts must not, however, be confused with those in Western terminology. A Vietminh front was created for a precise tactical mission in a clearly defined area of action, and placed under a commander who was given the means to do the job, including both regular units and such regional and popular troops in the zone of action as were capable of doing auxiliary work and giving logistic help. After the operation, the front was usually disbanded. The Vietminh also attached great importance to what they called "preparing the battlefield," that is to say, to the time-consuming task of assembling stockpiles, gathering intelligence, and sometimes building fortifications. Lastly, they were fond of paperwork: Many French officers have remarked on the incredible number of copies of messages, orders, and instructions that were issued. For all these reasons, the Vietminh needed even more time than might have been expected for the planning of large campaigns. Only for small, regiment-size operations were they able to plan and act very quickly, and even then the effective use of surprise often made it appear as though they had moved faster than they in fact had.

The remaining seven bureaus of the General Staff of 1953 consisted of directorates for Intelligence, Training, Administration, Armed Forces, Popular Troops, Military Affairs, and Communications and Liaison. In addition, there were a special Engineer and Artillery Section (suggesting the expected arrival of engineering equipment and artillery in ever greater amounts), and a Code Bureau. The main supply and maintenance functions had been taken away from the General Staff and, after the Chinese example, had been placed under a separate organization. The new staff was superior in training and experience to the General Staff of 1950. It was able to control the actions of several divisions, and proved that it could plan and execute operations of the size and scope of Dien Bien Phu.

The High Command now assumed the role of field army headquarters and staff as well as that of the highest military planning unit. It combined the functions of air force headquarters, air staff, a training command, and numbered air forces (or, in American army terms, the duties of the general staff, Continental Army Command, and field armies). As the regular army remained relatively small (about the size of a U.S. field army), this combination of tasks was not so difficult as it might seem at first glance. Furthermore, shortages of trained personnel probably rendered this concentration of direction and responsibility essential.

THE REGULAR UNITS

Directly under the High Command, in its capacity as field army headquarters, were the regular units of the army. Until 1950, the largest unit had been the regiment, sometimes reinforced and called a "group." The rate of development from there on was such that, even without Chinese aid, line divisions would soon have been created. However, the substantial Chinese aid that began coming in during 1950 assured better equipment and speeded the formation of larger units. Toward the end of the war, there were six divisions and several regiments in North Annam.

The first Vietminh divisions (in 1950) were good-size units of approximately 15,000 men. They appear to have had a very high proportion of combat soldiers classified as assault troops and firepower troops, and to have contained relatively small command and service elements. But the organizational charts are somewhat misleading, for, as will be shown below, the combat units included extraordinarily large numbers of supply soldiers.

Almost immediately, however, the Vietminh began to reduce the size of the division quite significantly, from about 15,000 men in 1950 to about 9,500 in 1953. Ostensibly, these smaller divisions were better for the war of movement, but one suspects that another reason may have compelled these reductions: After the costly battles of 1951 and early 1952, the Vietminh may actually have been short of men who were well enough trained to be in the front-line divisions.

Savings in manpower—some real and some illusory—were brought about by organizational changes and certain other factors. The early artillery units showed an unbelievably high ratio of men to weapons; for instance, a heavy-mortar (120-mm.) company, equipped with two pieces, had about 200 men! Though the weapon weighed only about 600 pounds, there were 80 porters per weapon. Again, a 75-mm.–artillery battalion armed with four pieces had nearly 1,100 men, of whom half were porters. The arrival of trucks was the biggest step toward solving the ammunition-supply problem, though to a limited degree the reductions in manpower may be attributed to improved training of the men. Another apparent reduction in the size of infantry divisions was the result of removing their artillery units and concentrating them in one heavy division. And finally, wherever possible, civilian labor was used to replace soldiers.

Over 90 percent of the personnel of the new, lighter division were members of its three regiments, leaving only about 1,000 men to be distributed over headquarters, the engineers, the liaison service, and the headquarters guards. By Western standards, therefore, the division was not capable of sustained combat. True, the lack of motor transport and other modern equipment reduced the need for service troops, just as the habit of living off the country reduced personal-supply needs. Despite the fact that these shortcomings in some ways proved to be hidden assets, the Vietminh believed that all considerations were outweighed by the advantages of having a modern army, which they continued to try to build.

The first heavy division (the 351st), formed in 1953, though its subordinate units had existed for some time, is believed to have had two artillery regiments, one engineer regiment, some transportation elements, and probably antiaircraft units. The independent regiments were largely assault troops, but most of them had recoilless weapons and mortars. Separate AA units, armed with 20-mm. and 40-mm. guns, did not appear until the last months of the war. There were no tank units, although some soldiers had received armored training in Chinese schools. Some special units (e.g., radio intercept) existed as early as 1950, but, in general, the Vietminh were weak in this field.

THE REGIONAL TROOPS

The High Command, in addition to its control of the regular army, exercised command over the territorial military organizations, with their regional and popular forces. The fullest and most efficient territorial organizations were those of North Annam and Tonkin, the strongholds of the Vietminh. They were set up as follows: The highest territorial unit was the interzone, which, in theory, included several zones. In practice, there were certain independent zones directly under the High Command, and some interzones without subordinate zones. Below the interzones or zones came the provinces, which were composed of several districts. At the base of the organization were the intervillages (several villages combined for administrative purposes) and the villages.

The Executive and Resistance Committee, sometimes called just Committee of Resistance, directed the overall war effort of interzone or zone. It dealt not only with the political, economic, and military aspects of the war but also with local problems of health and culture. One of its members was at the same time the military commander of the interzone and thus took orders from both the High Command and the Committee of Resistance. The local direction of military activities for the area lay with a command committee, composed of the interzone commander, his political counselor, and his adjutant, who were assisted by a staff. The commander and his committee were responsible for recruiting and supply functions; they were in charge of all the regional troops and any detached regular units in their area, and supervised the subordinate territorial commands.

The provincial command, under its own Committee of Resistance, was somewhat less elaborate than the inter-zone organization and commanded the subordinate district units as well as the provincial battalion. It was composed of a command section supported by a simple staff, with an office for operations and training, one for communications, and an intelligence section. This committee also had some logistic responsibilities.

The district, in turn, had its own Committee of Resistance, which was expected to raise a company of regional troops. Though similar in organization to that of the province, it was even less complex. A command committee consisted of the commander, his deputy, and a Party representative. "Technical cells" reported to the Committee on military intelligence, special espionage, political affairs, propaganda, arms production, communications, and administration. But as the districts were often inefficiently run or poorly organized, the province tended to assume greater powers than would appear from the theoretical organization.

THE POPULAR TROOPS

At the lowest echelon of the military organization was the village, with its individual fighters or small units of popular troops. The importance of these irregular troops should not be minimized; they were the backbone of the Vietminh military organization, as reflected in the very existence of a Directorate of Popular Troops at the ministry level, and of Committees on Popular Troops at the province and district levels. The Vietminh's effort to organize the entire population for the war effort was realized in the villages. The so-called popular troops consisted of two groups: the *Dan Quan,* composed of persons of both sexes and all ages who performed auxiliary military duties, and the *Dan Quan du Kich,* made up of men between the ages of eighteen and forty-five who were part-time guerrillas. The latter were organized into groups of from eight to fifteen men, who elected their leaders and were very lightly armed. In the strong areas, some villages had several such groups, which were combined into sections. There were also the *Dan Công,* civilian porters for the regular units.

The village and intervillage command was headed by a committee of three or four members (usually, though not always, including a Party representative for each village), and a secretary who tended to dominate the committee's affairs. The group directed the defense of the village and the day-to-day activities of the guerrillas. Very active villages often had a small supply of weapons and guerrilla material.

The foregoing description, as was pointed out above, applied chiefly to North Annam and Tonkin. In the south and in Laos and Cambodia, the territorial organization was less fully developed and far less effective. In 1947, the Vietminh established a regular command for the south under Nguyen Binh and virtually ignored Laos and Cambodia. But the long line of communications to the south and the apathetic or frankly unsympathetic attitude of much of the southern population made the task of the commander difficult, and the separate command was abolished in 1952. Nguyen Binh, whom the French described as an able leader, had personal ambitions and apparently tried to engage in large-scale warfare before he had developed a popular base. The circumstances surrounding his death in 1950 remain somewhat obscure, but it is generally believed that he was liquidated. Toward the end of the war, the Vietminh had developed some military organization in Laos, but there was still very little in Cambodia. In general, outside North Annam and Tonkin, their organization lacked continuity, cohesion, and efficiency.

REORGANIZATION

The distinctions among the three echelons of the military forces—the regular army, the regional troops, and the popular forces—were based on differences in training and equipment as well as of mission. It might be said that the three parts of this organization reflected the theory of the protracted war, with the popular forces representing the first period of guerrilla action, the regional forces paralleling the second stage, and the regular army dominating the third and final phase. And just as dividing lines between the stages of the war were sometimes indistinct, so also were the differences among these forces, especially those between the regular and the regional units.

Although the regular army was considered the ultimate weapon for victory, each of the three forces had an essential function to fulfill. As Giap stated, "We must concentrate the regular forces *and increase* the regional forces, or we shall make a false step." The regular army, or *chuluc,* was a precious unit, with a specific and crucial mission. Until 1950, this force, then still in its formative stage, was carefully husbanded, and it rarely engaged in combat when the issue was in doubt. In many of their operations, therefore, the French were unable to make contact with the regular forces but met instead the regional troops. By and large, the regular army was kept free to engage in the war of movement and to select both the field and the time for battle. Inasmuch as it was an elite unit and, of the three forces, had the best equipment, weapons, and uniforms as well as the highest pay, it was held strictly to its primary mission. Such duties as building fortifications and preparing the battlefield fell to the other two forces.

Slowly, and for the most part patiently, the Vietminh built up their infantry into a first-class force. After the precipitous 1946 engagements which ended in almost total defeat, they immediately began to reorganize and rebuild their battle corps, increasing both the number of units and the size and number of weapons in each.

An examination of Regiment 9, one of their best units but not an isolated case, shows the progress and growth that followed reorganization. In 1948, this regiment had six battalions, with a total of 1,800 men; it was equipped with only two mortars and two 75's, plus a few rapid-fire weapons. Three years later, it had only three battalions but 3,500 men, and possessed twenty-four mortars, nine recoilless cannon, eighteen machine guns, and over sixty rapid-fire weapons.

The following figures on regular and regional battalions show the Vietminh's overall military development in the three main regions between April, 1949, and June, 1951:

THE GROWTH OF VIETMINH REGULAR UNITS

| | April, 1949 | | June, 1951 | |
	Regular	Regional	Regular	Regional
Tonkin	20	50	78	6
Annam	7	43	21	6
Cochinchina	5	44	18	25
TOTALS	32	137	117	37

These figures reveal a striking increase in the number of regular units in all three areas, and a decline in the regional battalions that was particularly marked in Tonkin and Annam. Although there were almost as many units in the south as in the north, those in the south were smaller and of inferior quality. The steady expansion of the regular forces reflected in these figures may help one to understand why early 1951 could have appeared to Giap as the opportune moment at which to try his battle corps against the French in open battle—an attempt that caused him very heavy losses. The chart can be read, moreover, as reflecting the policy of taking regional forces into the regular army by unit without always replacing them. This development seems in curious contradiction to Giap's own fear that failure to increase the regional units might cause one to "make a false step." It might have been less serious in 1954, when the French were clearly on the defensive in the north and the need for regional troops consequently was less urgent. But in 1951, especially in the light of Giap's own statement, it can hardly have been a matter of preferred policy for the Vietminh. The only explanation that suggests itself, therefore, is that they were not free to choose, but were suffering from a shortage of men with whom to replace those advanced from regional to regular units.

The regional troops were less well organized, trained, and equipped than the regular forces. For the most part, the largest unit was the battalion, though in the latter stages of the war a few of the interzones had regiments. The men in the battalions and companies of regional troops were graduates of the popular forces, who had come in with the limited training that membership in the popular forces afforded. After further training in the regional troops, they advanced to the regular forces, individually or by unit—ideally when they were ready for it, but sometimes only because they were badly needed there. After the arrival of substantial Chinese aid, many of the units had uniforms and more equipment than before, but in general they continued to lack heavy weapons and equipment.

One of the primary duties of the regional forces was to protect an area and its population. They were the troops that met the French clearing operations, launched small attacks, and generally harassed the enemy; in short, they were the "mature guerrillas," who kept the enemy off balance and ambushed his reinforcements.

Their responsibilities extended both upward and downward in the total military organization. On the one hand, they trained and assisted the popular troops. On the other, they were what might be called the guardians of the regular army. Not only did they constitute a reserve and supply reinforcements to the regular forces when needed, but they prevented interference in the army's training and planning, prepared the battlefield for impending operations, protected the regular forces in retreat and advance, and took over some of their defensive missions.

The popular troops were divided into the two groups already mentioned: the *Dan Quan*, which theoretically included almost everyone, and the *Du Kich,* a smaller group that undertook guerrilla actions. The members of both groups served in their spare time, without interrupting their civilian tasks. The *Dan Quan* were essentially a labor force with a tinge of military training. Though occasionally they performed sabotage, their main responsibility was to collect intelligence, serve as guards, make road repairs, build bases, fortify the villages, and—very important—act as porters. They wore no uniforms and had virtually no weapons, except for some sabotage materials. The more selective *Du Kich* had some arms and undertook guerrilla actions on a small scale. They received rudimentary military training and were expected eventually to become line soldiers. Though generally forbidden to assemble in large groups, they were called together in emergencies when it was essential to prevent French clearing operations or to intensify guerrilla activity. Sometimes a few *Du Kich* were infiltrated into enemy-held villages, in order to prepare the way for a Vietminh assault.

But, important as the labor and guerrilla activities of the popular troops were, the Vietminh attributed still greater significance to their ideological mission. The major purpose of these troops was to lend the ideological war of the Vietminh the aspect of a national struggle in which the entire populace participated. The popular forces were also used to recruit young peasants for the military service of the Vietminh.

While apparently quite satisfied with the evolution and performance of the regular forces, Vietminh leaders seem to have felt less happy about the functioning of the territorial organization. At Party congresses and in messages to subordinate organizations, they frequently complained about the inefficiency and mistakes of the lower commands. Among other things, the lower echelons were said to change personnel too frequently: Men were assigned to different units every few months, with detriment to the stability and efficiency of the organization. Another charge was that interzone and provincial headquarters avored the technical cells over the combat units. The High Command admitted the importance of technical groups but insisted that they not be overemphasized at the expense of the fighting units. And finally, the territorial commands were constantly urged to make more efficient use of the population.

In 1952, Ho expressed some of the same misgivings in a severe lecture on the shortcomings of the Vietminh organization in general. The people, he said, were anxious and ready to serve, but they had not been used in the most rational and efficient manner. Furthermore, while noting the progress that had been made, Ho blamed the leaders for bureaucratic excesses and for the increase in waste and corruption (familiar charges in any Communist regime). Some of the cadres, he warned, were not sincerely practicing the principles of the Party and were retarding progress, and a few local leaders who nourished personal ambitions and deviationist tendencies would have to reform or be removed.

Aside from these defects in leadership and organization, the Vietminh had to grapple with certain inevitable problems inherent in the situation in Indochina, which made the formation and efficient operation of organizations difficult. As in any underdeveloped area, there was a shortage of trained personnel, technicians as well as administrators. For lack of lower-echelon administrators, the central administration tended to keep much of the power in its own hands and to issue incredibly detailed instructions to the lower levels. Not only did this severely curtail the initiative of lower officials, but it also put a great burden of time and labor on the top people. As time went on, however, the Vietminh succeeded in training new personnel and thus eliminating some of the worst bottlenecks.

Another serious obstacle to Viet progress was created by the minority groups, most of whom lived in the mountain areas. As mentioned earlier, these groups regarded the Vietminh as a Vietnamese government, and thus as one to be feared and distrusted. Though Giap had succeeded in overcoming some of these prejudices when he worked in the mountainous areas during World War II, he continued to meet a certain amount of opposition all through the revolutionary war. However, the French were slow to exploit their advantage in this respect. It was not until 1953 that they organized guerrilla groups in the mountains to strike at the Vietminh lines of communications. By that time, their dilatory tactics over the granting of independence and their inability to protect the minorities had lost them much of the latter's support.

Another difficulty for the Vietminh lay with the nationalists who were not Communists, yet whose support was essential if the war was to be won. Therefore, even as the Communists became stronger, they were careful to disguise or soft-pedal their purely Communist objectives and to emphasize nationalist and reform ideas to the general population. As late as 1952, when they clearly had control of the movement, they were still cautious about preaching pure Communism outside their own organization.

The Vietminh ultimately perfected an organization that allowed them to defeat the French, and they must be given their due for organizational achievement. Yet there were flaws in the operation of the system, and the speeches of Ho and others testify to the presence of internal difficulties. In dealing with many of these problems, the Vietminh were aided by the inertia and inflexibility of the French. There were opposition groups, for example, whom the French, had they been alert to the situation, might well have used effectively to weaken the Vietminh. Also, if the French had been quicker to recognize the tremendous surge of nationalism and the opportunity it afforded them to meet the demand for independence in good faith, they could have increased the difficulties of the Vietminh many times. Even as late as 1950, many Vietnamese were willing to give the French a chance to show that they meant to stand by their statements in favor of independence for Vietnam, but the French continued to procrastinate. Vietnamese nationalists were thus slowly discredited and forced into the Vietminh camp. It was similar with the potentially strong opposition of the minorities in the mountain areas. Here again, French procrastination, lack of understanding of the needs of these groups, and evidence, now and then, of French duplicity eventually turned those minorities to the Vietminh. With this failure to exploit all opportunities for undermining the Viet organization and movement through political and psychological action, the prospects of a French military victory became more and more remote.

NOTES

1. In 1951, Ho Chi Minh announced the creation of the Lao Dong (Workers') Party, essentially the first overt appearance of the Communist Party since its "dissolution" in 1945.

2. See pp. 18–19.

Chapter 3

VIETMINH PERSONNEL AND LOGISTICS

Few regimes have emphasized as strongly as the Vietminh the importance of the total mobilization of the populace. The constitution of 1946 provided for universal military conscription, and in 1949 the government actually ordered the draft. In practice, however, it did not prove feasible, for the Vietminh government was far from having the bureaucratic machinery necessary to put such a law into effect. Recruiting for the Vietminh army, therefore, remained informal. By the end of the war, Vietminh forces numbered about 300,000 men, a small percentage of the estimated 28 million total population of Vietnam. It is true that the Vietminh controlled the less populous sections of the country; but, on the other hand, they were able to draw many of their recruits from French-held areas.

RECRUITMENT

Since no attempt at conscription was really ever made, the Vietminh have always claimed that the men who served had volunteered. In fact, the Vietminh put great effort into sporadic recruiting campaigns, which combined pressure with propaganda and enticement. It is known that some young men were forcibly dragged into the armed forces, and that in other cases indirect pressure was brought to bear on families or village leaders to supply recruits. Usually, strong-arm and other pressure methods were accompanied by propaganda appeals to the prospective recruits to serve their country against the European imperialists and for the betterment of society. Openly Communistic appeals were generally avoided. Inducements for those who joined included the promise of improved living conditions and a general education. Deserters and prisoners of war were accepted after careful political indoctrination, but their number always remained small.

The motives of the men freely joining the armed forces of the Vietminh were probably often mixed and cannot be determined accurately. Certainly patriotism and, in some cases, Communist beliefs were the dominant motivations. In other instances, the attraction of good food and clothing and possible future education may have been the incentives. The lure of adventure and escape from a dreary life probably caused some to join. A French poll of Viet prisoners of war attempted to discover why they had joined the army. In this group, 38 per cent stated that they believed in the Vietminh cause; 25 per cent expressed resentment at having been forced into the army against their wishes; 23 per cent indicated that they, too, had been compelled to join, but did not seem to resent the use of force; finally, 6 per cent had felt the army provided an interesting career. The survey results should be judged with reservations, because those captured probably constituted the least reliable and most poorly indoctrinated of the army and hence were not a fully representative segment. Periodically, the Vietminh seemed to suffer shortages of man—power—an indication that their means of compulsion and persuasion were not wholly successful. (Women volunteers made up only a small minority of the army's total strength.)

Through their prisoners, the French also sought to discover the social composition of the Vietminh forces. The results of the inquiry showed that 46 per cent of the army was composed of peasants and laborers, with laborers in the majority. (It is not clear why the French did not classify these two groups separately.) According to the prisoners, 48 per cent were petty officials, and the remaining 6 per cent came from miscellaneous professions and trades. The petty officials thus constituted nearly half the army, although peasants made up the majority of the population. It should be noted that the French controlled most of the urban areas where most petty officials lived. The percentages seem to suggest that these officials were more attracted by Communist propaganda than were the peasants, who were also exposed to the Vietminh terror tactics. It is likely, however, that these French statistics apply to headquarter and elite groups, not the line units.

Recruiting began at the village level. The Viets attempted to organize the people of every village and group of villages into part-time semimilitarized workers for the Vietminh war effort. Although these people were neither in uniform nor actually part of the military forces, they were potential soldiers. Once they had been politically indoctrinated and had received some very rudimentary discipline, they graduated to the village guerrilla cell and from there to the regional forces.

TRAINING

Training varied not only in the three types of forces, but with the different echelons in each. The popular forces, or guerrillas, had a self-training program, with assistance from the regional troops and occasional aid from noncoms and officers of the regular army. Their training was largely political, but it included some instruction in the use of personal weapons, as well as lessons in sabotage. Some of the more advanced village units had close-order drill and even instruction on automatic weapons. At the district level, companies underwent additional training, with continued emphasis on individual arms, more instruction in the use of automatic weapons, and elementary-education in small-unit tactics.

The members of the regional units usually were graduates of the popular forces and thus had had some of the training outlined above. Once they joined the regional forces, they received more individual instruction and began to study unit tactics. Regular army officers assigned to the regional units provided the formal training. In addition, "regional schools" instructed soldiers in the use of the more difficult weapons and in special skills and lower-level staff duties. During this phase of training, the individual not only gained considerable military knowledge but had the opportunity to experience combat and to learn to adapt himself to military life. From these regional troops were eventually chosen the members of the regular army. The process of rising through this system often took several years.

Up to this point, the irregular fighter's training had been sporadic and had in most cases suffered from a lack of weapons and a shortage of instructors. But as soon as he graduated to the regular army, he was exposed to formal and intensive discipline under highly trained Vietminh officers and often Chinese instructors. Moreover, he received a uniform, individual weapons, and better food and equipment.

Upon entering the regular army, the soldier was obliged to take a ten-point oath, in which he swore (1) to sacrifice everything for the good of the cause; (2) to obey his officers completely; (3) to fight resolutely and without complaint; (4) to train diligently; (5) to keep secrets; (6) to bear torture if captured; (7) never to reveal information; (8) to take care of his equipment; (9) to respect and help the civilian population; and (10) to maintain high morale. The oath was not only the soldier's guide as to what was expected of him, but also an indication of the Vietminh's chief points of concern. The fact that two of the ten points dealt with security or the preservation of the "secret" reveals that even the sternly indoctrinated Vietminh soldiers, like men in other armies, could not resist the temptation to tell what their unit was going to do. Morale seemed to be another special concern, and the wording of point 9 underlined the close association of the soldier with the civilian population.

Beyond the requirement of the oath, reminders of the virtues and qualities of the Viet soldier were part of the men's training. A captured document—*The Popular Army of Vietnam*—which originated with the Office of Propaganda and Instruction, contains a lesson-by-lesson outline of a typical indoctrination course. It lists such obvious prerequisites as bravery, patriotism, and the willing acceptance of military discipline, and further demands of every soldier an endeavor to serve the people, to acquire the proper political ideas, and to improve himself in all ways. In addition, the manual calls on each man to have feeling and affection for his fellow soldiers, and literally concludes with the statement: "The army is one great happy family."

Vietminh leaders always maintained that their soldiers fought willingly and happily. In practice, despite their condemnation of discipline in the enemy army, the Vietminh themselves insisted on very strict discipline. But as the above-mentioned manual explained, whereas discipline was tyrannical in the imperialist armies, it was good and proper in the Vietminh army. Communist discipline, according to the pamphlet, was self-imposed, and assured the proper political indoctrination of the soldiers and thus the efficient functioning of the liberation forces.

Since the Vietminh considered infantry the decisive arm of combat, all soldiers received at least basic infantry training. Close-order drill developed precision and quick response to orders; instruction on such personal infantry weapons as rifle, grenade, and bayonet followed. Great emphasis was placed on camouflage and personal protection, and a considerable amount of time was spent on terrain studies and methods of geographic orientation.

Some soldiers were trained as assault troops and were strictly riflemen; others were slated to become members of the firepower or support elements and were, therefore, concerned with heavier weapons, i.e., machine guns, bazookas, recoilless rifles, and mortars. Careful and intensive training was provided on these weapons, and the Vietminh soldier developed great skill in their use, particularly in the handling of recoilless rifles and mortars, which, particularly in the early stages of the war, took the place of artillery.

Once the soldier had become competent with weapons and familiar with small-unit tactics, he was taught largerunit tactics and the intricacies of maneuvering with heavy-weapon support. Battalion and regimental assault tactics were rehearsed over and over, often with models of French posts and forts simulating the objectives, until the soldier knew his role so well that it had become practically automatic. Actually, however, unit tactics never became as rigid as this might indicate but were adapted to specific situations.

A small portion of the soldiers' time was devoted to obtaining a general education. Many of the recruits were illiterate, and the army provided their first basic schooling and even offered some courses in literature and philosophy.

In the course of the war, the Vietminh developed an extensive school system, partly in Vietnam and partly in Red China. There were schools for the various weapons, and two schools—at Ha Giang and Bac Kan—trained officers for regimental duty. Even before the Red Chinese reached the border, some men had been trained in the Communist-held areas of China, and a few had been trained by the Chinese Nationalists. However, as the Vietminh began to form regiments and to think in terms of division-size forces, their training needs grew. Red China provided schools for noncommissioned, company-grade, and staff officers. Particularly welcomed by the Vietminh were the schools for specialists, who were desperately needed for the more modern army that was being formed: Engineers were trained at the engineers' school at Nanning, while tank troops studied at the armored school at Wu Ming, both in China. Reportedly, some men went to China for pilot training, although the Vietminh never had an air force. It has been estimated that, by the time of the cease-fire, in 1954, up to 40,000 Vietminh soldiers had received training in Red China. In addition to providing school facilities, the Chinese also sent a large number of instructors to Indochina for duty with the staff and regular units and, in some cases, with the territorial commands.

The most important aspect of the soldiers' training, however, and that which consumed the most time, was the political. Its two objectives were to produce politically reliable and enthusiastic soldiers and to provide effective propaganda agents. (Giap stated repeatedly that the soldier's work as a political agent was at least equal in importance to his duty as a fighter.) The opportunities for agents were varied and many, since regular units frequently lived among the people and infiltrated enemy-held areas. The custom of assigning regular-army men to duty with the regional and popular forces also furnished wide opportunity for indoctrination.

The aforementioned manual on *The Popular Army of Vietnam* tells a good deal about the nature of the soldiers' political indoctrination and reveals the themes that were stressed most heavily. It begins with a brief history of the army, to which, significantly, it refers as the "troops of propaganda and liberation." This thought is restated in the definition of the army's two principal missions as being, first, to spread propaganda in order to win people to the cause and to gain recruits, and, second, to wage the armed struggle against the enemy. The main arguments of the pamphlet are that the French have deprived the Vietnamese of their independence as well as their individual liberties, and that the tyranny of imperialism must be smashed. There are only subtle and minor references to Communist aims, though the Communist Workers' Party *(Dang Lao Dong)* is praised for its effective leadership.

A favorite Communist device—self-criticism—was widely used in political training. Captured Vietminh material is full of such self-critiques, painstakingly written by semi-literate soldiers who had been forced to look back into their lives and to confess any crimes they might have committed against society. These reports went into considerable detail and covered all facets of life. One young soldier, for example, admitted that he had stolen some rice at the age of six and had, in later years, been selfish in his dealings with other members of the village. The moral was always that one must be willing to sacrifice oneself for the welfare of society.

The large amount of time and careful planning devoted to political indoctrination brought results. There is no question that the Vietminh were able to create a large and dedicated army. Desertions were very rare, and morale problems relatively few.[1]

MEDICAL SERVICES

In this underdeveloped country there naturally were few doctors, and certainly not enough to answer the needs of the armed forces. However, the Vietminh attempted to provide medical service for their regular units. Their goal was an ambitious one: About half a mile from the battlefield there was to be a collection point where all the wounded men would be assembled and given a cursory examination. At a sorting area, about three to six miles from the front, doctors would separate the more seriously wounded from the slightly injured and evacuate them to a hospital some five to ten miles farther to the rear. (The hopeless cases would not be moved and would be left to die.) Approximately twelve to twenty miles from the front, there was to be an operating hospital. In practice, nothing like this existed. However, every regular division had a medical company, usually with at least one doctor, and maintained an evacuation and hospital service. In several of the Viet-held areas there were recuperation points. By the time of the cease-fire, the Chinese had sent large amounts of medical supplies to Indochina, but they had not been able to train the necessary medical personnel, or spare enough of their own, to supply the Vietminh with an adequate, well-functioning organization. Medical service for the regional and popular forces was virtually nonexistent and at best very primitive.

COMMUNICATIONS AND LOGISTCS

There is little precise information on the Vietminh communication system. Viet leaders were quick to recognize the importance of communications, and early in the war tried to purchase radios from foreign countries and to repair captured or abandoned Japanese equipment. At the beginning, before the advent of massive Chinese aid, the great diversity of equipment complicated the repair and maintenance problems, particularly in view of the shortage of trained technicians. The Vietminh did succeed in repairing the civilian telephone and telegraph lines of the country and using them for routine messages. But while they employed the civilian radio net, they were anxious to develop their own military network as far as possible. By the end of the war, thanks to Chinese aid, even units as small as companies and platoons had at least one radio and were thus in communication with their adjacent units and higher headquarters. Semaphore units were used at times, and messengers remained a very important element of the communication system. There was also an elaborate system of runners with relay stations.

Throughout the war, on the other hand, the Vietminh was troubled by the various phases of logistics—the production, acquisition, and transportation of arms, food, and equipment. They had started out with some Japanese equipment, part of it stolen and the rest freely given at the time of the Japanese surrender. Some matériel had also been parachuted to them by the Allies during the fight against the Japanese. Early in the war, a considerable amount of equipment was shipped from Thailand to the Vietminh, but in 1948, a change in Thai foreign policy closed off this supply. Nationalist China sent aid by land and sea (even though the French ostensibly had control of the sea),[2] and some matériel came from the Philippines. With the exception of what had been acquired from Japan, most of the equipment was of American make. Other matériel was captured or stolen from the French in the course of the war. Indeed, the Vietminh set up a price scale for such stolen equipment, by which they were willing to pay up to three hectares of national land for certain special items.

Local production was a major source of arms and equipment. Many small shops, employing from ten to fifteen workers, would operate in a given area. Partly or wholly mobile, they could be moved from place to place according to the threat of the French advance. These shops made the crudest sort of equipment, with manpower often the only source of energy and automobile motors and simple engines available only at times. Some workshops limited themselves to making mines and explosives, which were used heavily by the guerrillas. Production in these workshops was geared to local needs, and even at the end of the war, there were few factories producing for nationwide consumption. A notable exception was the manufacture of bazookas, which was centered entirely in the Tonkin area. The larger shops and factories (employing up to 500 persons) were more or less permanently located in firmly held Vietminh bases.

There were few factories in the south, though small and dispersed shops existed in the Plaine des Joncs, Cochinchina. Cambodia also had some important shops near Ampil, but Laos had virtually none.

Despite the shortage of precision tools, power, and raw materials, the Vietminh managed to produce fairly large quantities of materials. In the first six months of 1948, for instance, the Viets reported that shops in one intersector produced 38,000 grenades, 30,000 rifle cartridges, 8,000 cartridges for light machine guns, 60 rounds for a bazooka, and 100 mines. Another sector produced 61 light machine guns, 4 submachine guns, 20 automatic pistols, and 7,000 cartridges in the entire year 1948. Besides manufacturing, some of these shops excelled in repairing and modifying weapons. None of them, of course, was able to produce any heavy equipment, though one factory in Tonkin was making 120-mm. mortars as early as 1949.

Only with the arrival of Chinese aid did the logistical problems of the Vietminh begin to be solved. According to reliable estimates, petroleum products and munitions comprised 75 per cent of Chinese aid, while the remaining 25 per cent consisted of arms and medical and signal equipment. Though the precise extent of Chinese aid is not known, the following figures seem to be generally accepted: In 1951, the rate of aid from China was about 10 to 20 tons per month. By the end of 1952, the flow had risen to 250 tons, and in 1953, it averaged between 400 and 600 tons. At the beginning of the assault on Dien Bien Phu, Chinese aid was said to be up to 1,500 tons a month, and by June, 1954, it reportedly had reached 4,000 tons.

It has been estimated that 75 per cent of Chinese supplies entered Indochina at Ta Lung and went by way of Cao Bang, Nguyen Binh, Bac Kan, and Thai Nguyen to Vietminh in the west or around the French-held Delta to forces in the south. A secondary route led from Pinghsiang in China to Dong Dang, Lang Son, and from there by poorer roads to Thai Nguyen. Two other entrance points, Lao Kay and Ban Nam Cuong, were considered of little importance. The Chinese had built a railroad to the Indochina border in the east, but there was none to take the goods from the border into Indochina. Materials, therefore, had to be stored whenever the Viet transport schedule fell behind, particularly after supply routes had been hard hit by air attack.

In this underdeveloped country, with its one or two railways and few roads, transportation was bound always to pose a problem, and to the very end of the war, the coolies were its mainstay. The Vietminh organized what they called the "auxiliary service," which was essentially a labor force of local inhabitants. It provided transportation facilities by coolies and whatever equipment was available. In an attempt to control this organization closely, the Vietminh allowed only certain units or headquarters—such as the General Staff, the General Directorate of Food, interzone commands, and other high echelons—to call on its services. The auxiliary force was organized in groups of 15 men each, with 3 groups making up a section and 3 sections a company. With this simple organization, the Vietminh accomplished almost incredible logistical feats.

Logistics experts had drawn up tables showing what could be expected from this primitive transportation system. For instance, on the plains or on reasonably level land with few obstacles, the coolies were expected to do 15.5 miles per day (12.4 at night) carrying 55 lbs. of rice or from 33 to 44 lbs. of arms. In mountainous areas, the day's march was shortened to about 9 miles, or 7.5 miles at night, and the load was reduced to 28.6 lbs. of rice and 22 to 33 lbs. of arms. It was estimated that buffalo carts could carry approximately 770 lbs. and travel about 7.5 miles per day, while a horse cart could carry only 473 lbs. but could travel about 12.4 miles a day. The Vietminh made important use of mule companies, and also of bicycles, which were loaded with as much as 150 pounds and pushed by coolies. Wherever possible, they also took advantage of the waterways.

After the Chinese Communists had reached the border, the Vietminh slowly built up their motor transport, and it was estimated that by 1953, they had a total of close to 1,000 trucks. About a third of these were organized into Regiment 16. This unit, whose task it was to carry supplies from the border to the main depots, was divided into 9 companies, each with 90 to 100 men and approximately 35 trucks. The 9 companies operated independently of one another, rather than in the motor-pool fashion of the American army. This was dictated by the fact that the French air force, in its attempts to interdict the supply system, had succeeded in cutting a number of bridges, and the Vietminh did not have the engineers to repair these bridges rapidly enough, so that the area of supply and communication had been cut into a number of segments. The Vietminh simply put a truck company of Regiment 16 into each of these segments, which thereupon became a self-sufficient transportation sector, with its own gasoline stocks, supplies, and repair shops. Though this system involved innumerable transfers of equipment, the plentiful supply of manpower enabled it to operate successfully.

As the need arose for new roads or supplementary routes, the Vietminh marshaled the necessary labor force and constructed them. Thus, in the late fall of 1953, a road was built from Tuan Giao to a point near Dien Bien Phu to assure the delivery of supplies for the impending battle.

While this primitive use of manpower yielded results, it caused a serious drain on the available labor force. One Vietminh division, in a simple operation, is estimated to have required about 40,000 porters to supply its minimum needs. When one remembers that these divisions had very little heavy equipment and were not motorized (thus requiring no POL[3]), this was an enormous support force. One of the obvious reasons for the staggering number of porters was the fact that, in addition to army supplies, the porters had to carry their personal provisions. And especially where the lines of communication were long, the coolies' own supplies often made up the bulk of their burden. However, there were advantages to this primitive system. Coolies were not only plentiful, but able to travel cross-country, and their easily concealed columns were almost immune to air attack.

NOTES

1. One major exception was the period of low morale after the Vietminh defeats early in 1951. See p. 11.

2. As recalled in the Introduction, the Chinese Nationalists, after the Japanese surrender in World War II, agreed with the Allies to occupy northern Vietnam, ostensibly to hold that territory until the French were able to return to Indochina. Actually, however, the Chinese were not unwilling to help the Vietminh. They had designs on the harbor of Haiphong, important to Chinese commerce, and indeed had hopes of replacing the French, or at least of retaining control of the Tonkin area. Hence they played the Vietminh off against the French.

3. Petroleum, Oil, and Lubricants.

Chapter 4

VIETMINH OPERATIONS
AND TACTICS

A broad political objective underlay the Vietminh's tactics, as it did their strategy. Where Western war aims were merely to occupy a certain territory or to break the will of the enemy, the Viet revolutionaries wanted to win the support or gain control of the populace. In their tactical teachings, they continually emphasized that the goal of an attack was not alone to destroy a given French post but to liberate the inhabitants in the surrounding area and gain their support. "Some of our cadres harbor the mistaken idea," said Giap in 1952, "that armed deeds constitute the only mission of armed forces. They do not focus attention on serving the plan of total conflict and especially propaganda." He went on to complain that this misconception in Vietminh quarters had allowed the enemy to make progress in his propaganda in some areas where the population remained sympathetic to the French, and Viet recruiting, intelligence, and other activities had been correspondingly hampered.

On the strictly military plane, a study of the Vietminh's successes suggests that they rested chiefly on three interrelated factors: (1) a set of five simple tactical principles; (2) full, accurate, and up-to-date intelligence; and (3) detailed planning.

PRINCIPLES AND PREREQUISITES

The Vietminh taught five principles of tactics. The first of these was speed of movement in all phases of combat. Forces were to concentrate quickly, take positions at once, and not linger in any one area. They usually would start from a given point and march for two or three nights to the area of attack, creating a strong element of surprise for the French, who were not aware of the direction of the Viet movements. The position would be developed in one night, and the attack launched in the very early morning. In pursuit, speed was perhaps even more important. "Once the enemy is disorganized," wrote Giap, "it is necessary to ignore fatigue in order automatically to begin the pursuit without awaiting orders." He cited the lack of vigor in the fall campaign of 1950 as a case in which Viet troops had not been sufficiently imbued with motivation for the enemy's total destruction and had thus wasted the sacrifices already made. Giap went further than American doctrine in being willing, if necessary, to forgo reorganization after battle, for he considered it more important to seek to overtake the enemy at once and to continue striking him. If Giap's approach was successful, this was attributable partly to his troops' intense desire to annihilate the enemy (rather than conquer a given piece of terrain). But in part it was due to the fact that the Viet army, being essentially an infantry body, was relatively simple in structure, and reorganization therefore was not a great problem. In retreat, too, speed was all-important. First of all, the Vietminh emphasized, one must never be caught without a way of retreat. The way might be either a definite line from the battle area or a plan by which soldiers would melt into the population and "disappear," sometimes individually and sometimes in small groups. Troops thus dispersed were either reconcentrated later or were left to sustain and aid the guerrillas of the area, depending on the situation.

Surprise, the second principle of Viet tactics, combined the elements of speed, secrecy, and the choice of unsuspected objectives. A favorite device, "intoxication of the enemy," involved a series of deliberate deceptions. The Viet side would deliberately leak information to the enemy that would mislead him into expecting an attack in a certain place at a certain time. To this end, they would make up fake documents and plant them on double agents and on persons who apparently had "rallied" to the French cause. The numerical designation of regular units would be attached to regional units in order to confuse the French. All units would be moved back and forth to give an impression of the movement of large numbers. As mentioned before, night marches that avoided villages and inhabited areas were another means of creating surprise. In a large-scale campaign, all these devices might be employed in combination.

Another tactical principle was to undermine enemy morale in every way possible. Viet agents were infiltrated into French camps to encourage treason and spread propaganda. Also, the Vietminh did not hesitate to make threats against pro-French families. Although Giap was rather reluctant to pay bribes or to use women for black-mail and bribery, these means were not always neglected. As a general rule, the Vietminh would attack only if the manpower ratio was in their favor, but they believed that with the right combination of surprise and ruse, a highly disciplined small outfit could often prevail over a larger force. They would rely on those means in exceptional circumstances, but only when they felt certain of being able thereby to offset a shortage in manpower.

Much thought was given to security for the Viet forces. Speciai intelligence units, whose functions were much broader than, for example, those of American intelligence units, played the role of security and reconnaissance forces, and were used to screen regular forces as well as to cover them. They also infiltrated the enemy front to gain information on the preparedness and morale of the enemy. Regional and popular troops were used to protect the regular forces and permit them to fight under the most advantageous conditions. Regional and popular forces, in turn, were covered by small groups with little formal organization, in fact, by the local inhabitants.

The last principle of tactics called for the collaboration of the populace in all military actions. The paradox here is that support from the people was no longer merely an aim of Viet tactics but an integral part of them. A monthly report of the 80th Regiment re-emphasized the importance of this principle by stating that the aim of regimental attacks was not so much to take French posts as to gain control over the population. The 80th Regiment, although part of the regular forces, was detached to a territorial command, and its report specified further that the *raison d'être* of the guerrilla unit, no matter what its size, was to establish and maintain a political-military organization in its area, which formed a basis for regular operations. Giap elaborated on this point in a September, 1952, directive:

> In order to intensify guerrilla activity our attention must be focused not only on the regional troops but also on the armed bases of the communes and the communal guerrillas. The principal question is that of popular troops and the guerrillas. In certain regions one strives to reinforce these troops but is faced with great difficulties. The morale of the population [there] is not as solid as elsewhere. The bases of the popular troops and the cells of the party have been largely annihilated by the enemy and no longer present a satisfactory situation. These armed bases cannot perform their activities and are safeguarded only with great difficulty. Thus, our mission of first priority is to reinforce the popular bases.

On another occasion Giap remarked:

> Guerrilla [warfare] is an armed struggle of all classes of the people. As long as the people do not have a strong hate of the enemy in their hearts, do not have an energetic fighting spirit, as long as the mechanism of the regional authority and the action of the party are not based on a solid organization, one is not able to create a movement for a large battle or for intensified guerrilla action.

In the Vietminh instructions for *Dich Van* groups that have infiltrated enemy-held areas, there is the sentence: "It is the duty of those who are in the enemy zone to create action around them, to strike the enemy with precision and speed wherever he is, destroying all opponents and appropriating stocks and materiel, and resorting to ambush, attacks, and other measures that create disorder and discontent."

The office of the political commissar for every unit had its propaganda section in charge of psychological warfare. It prepared pamphlets and newspapers for distribution to the civilian population as well as the troops and worked out topics for the propaganda effort of the individual soldier.

A propaganda instruction to the troops that were to invade Laos in 1953 reflects the main themes of Vietminh propaganda directed toward inhabitants of the mountain areas. Beginning with the usual condemnation of French imperialists and their desire to keep all the races of Indochina in slavery, the document goes on to stress the brotherhood of these races and their common cause against colonialism. Ho is portrayed as a kindly and forgiving leader, untiringly working for national independence and the good of all peoples. The propaganda instruction furthermore suggests stressing the army's love for the people and the people's affection for the army, and supplies a long list of ways in which the people might help the army. Reassurance to the natives takes the form of helpful hints on air shelters and other self-defense measures, as well as the promise that on the rare occasions when the army is short of food, the government will pay well for any supplies seized by the troops.

INTELLIGENCE AND RECONNAISSANCE

Not only a careful propaganda plan but painstaking and detailed intelligence coverage formed part of the preparation of every Vietminh operation. Prior to 1948, there were only a *Sûreté* and a Political Intelligence Service, but their findings were not always readily available to the High Command. In response to the growing need for a purely military, operational intelligence service, the *Quan Bao* (Military Intelligence) was formed about 1948.

An elite corps within the army, the *Quan Bao* was composed of Party members who had been especially chosen for their physical, mental, and moral qualifications. After their selection, the recruits went through three months of special training in schools that frequently changed location. Each school had a total of about 150 students. The courses were broadly conceived, and students were subjected to physical conditioning and self-defense, sensory training, background information on the French, and reconnaissance work. As the intelligence corps was also the reconnaissance element of the Vietminh army, the schools placed special stress on the refinement of the physical senses, and future agents were taught to improve their hearing in order to determine not only the direction of a noise but their own distance from it, and learn to distinguish the dominant from lesser noises. Students also learned to observe very quickly and to gauge weight without measuring aids. The course included a whole system of helpful tricks, some of them as elementary as putting an ear to the ground to detect noises, or breathing out before speaking in order to make the voice lower and more distinct. Agents were also instructed in ways to disguise their feelings and were shown how to improve their memory. They learned to write accurate and complete reports, which would give the source as well as the time and circumstances of the matter reported and would include an evaluation by the agent.

After this training, intelligence recruits were assigned to their units. Usually, these were divided into the *Quan Bao,* concerned with intelligence in a narrow sense, and the *Trinh Sat,* responsible for reconnaissance. Companies and battalions had only small *Trinh Sat* units; at regiment and division level, however, there would be intelligence companies, each of which included one *Quan Bao* section and two *Trinh Sat* sections. The *Quan Bao* was the directing element, which planned and co-ordinated the intelligence effort, utilized the information gathered, and for the most part supplied the intelligence officers for the territorial commands and the General Staff.

While the intelligence service employed such comparatively modern methods as radio intercept and triangulation as means of obtaining information, it counted heavily on direct personal interrogation of both the local civilians and enemy personnel, and its training schools therefore emphasized the value of obtaining prisoners. Special groups, organized to launch attacks for the express purpose of capturing prisoners, usually comprised four subsections: a fire group, which was to cause confusion in the enemy ranks; a capturing group, which rounded up the prisoners; a support group, which helped the capturing group and watched for reinforcements; and an escort group, which took the prisoners to the rear for interrogation. In addition to these more or less formal assaults, the Vietminh resorted also to ambush and surprise attacks on small units and tried to seize isolated soldiers wherever possible.

From all accounts, the Vietminh were psychologically very adept at interrogation. They would interview prisoners of war two or three times, for long periods at a stretch, and preferably at hours when the prisoners' resistance was lowest. They had been taught to be very objective, and to approach the prisoners without any show of preconceived ideas. A favorite practice was to employ irony or sarcasm, which tended to make the prisoner lose his patience and give out more information than he intended. Sometimes, Viet agents would be slipped into prisoners' cells or enclosures. According to accounts by French prisoners, the Vietminh seldom resorted to force.

As the war went on, intelligence units took over more and more, though not all, of the reconnaissance and security duties formerly performed by the regional and popular troops. At battalion, regiment, and division level, intelligence units provided cover for the movements of these forces as well as the reconnaissance for all operations. In the effort to obtain information they used all possible devices: they would disguise themselves to infiltrate enemy areas, send armed patrols to contact the enemy and ascertain the location of his positions, and engage in combat if it promised to yield valuable information.

Anyone familiar with United States army reconnaissance would recognize many of the Vietminh reconnaissance functions, but there were also some rather important differences. Responsible for the security of the troops, reconnaissance units reconnoitered both retreat and advance routes and searched for places suitable for ambush. Agents were planted in suspect zones to keep the units informed. Both the teaching and the execution of camouflage were among the functions of Viet reconnaissance. After combat, it was up to the reconnaissance units to discover what losses the Vietminh had suffered and what arms had been taken from the enemy. Also, at this point, they were responsible for recording their own mistakes, leading troops back to the concentration area, guarding the prisoners, and authorizing civilians to return to their homes armed with propaganda. For units in camp, they had to investigate the cooking areas, examine gifts from the local people, and keep a check on relations between troops and native population. It was their duty, furthermore, to guard automatic weapons as well as documents, to keep an eye on soldiers in public places, and to prevent desertion. On festive occasions, they were responsible for the behavior and discipline of the troops in town, at the same time that they had to post guards and lookouts for enemy aircraft and prepare for quick evacuation in case of attack.

Captured Vietminh documents have brought to light painstaking intelligence surveys of French troop dispositions, habits, and activities, which obviously served the Vietminh as a very good planning base for their operations. One intelligence study prepared by the Vietminh for their northwestern operations in 1952 impressed the French greatly by its scope as well as by the detail and accuracy of the information. The document included a very careful survey of the terrain and its trafficability for all types of vehicles and for coolies. It also contained an objective study of the various tribes in the area and their attitudes toward the Vietminh and the French. Part of this section was given over to a detailed description of the Vietminh's secret bases in the area and to a loyalty estimate of the people in them. In the Gia Hoi–Sai Luong base, for instance, ninety persons were marked down as Vietminh sympathizers, of whom thirty were regarded as completely reliable. Again, in the Phu Nhan–Son Thin area, there were twenty-five faithful adherents scattered through several villages. The study concluded by stating that, although these figures did not add up to strong popular support, the bases did offer a certain hospitality to the Vietminh troops.

THE INFANTRY AND THE MOBILITY FACTOR

Vietminh tactics were essentially infantry tactics. A significant amount of artillery became available only in the last months of the war, and armor was lacking throughout. But even had there been the heavy equipment that the Vietminh continued to wish for, armor and artillery obviously had very limited mobility in an underdeveloped country with the difficult terrain of Indochina. Furthermore, Giap realized that it was quicker and easier to turn a guerrilla into an infantryman than into a tanker or artilleryman.

The Viet army's heavy reliance on infantry meant, first of all, that their combat units were not encumbered with many tanks or much artillery and that the battle corps was more or less free of combat trains and heavy service units. The army was thus quite mobile and not tied to particular areas or bases. By the same token, it was not bound to stick to the roads, but could execute cross-country marches with considerable ease and speed and managed to perform great feats of infiltration. Finally, this primarily infantry army was able to escape detection and attack from the air.

Mobility—in offensive as well as defensive action—was the key to all operations, from the small actions of the guerrillas to the larger campaigns of the regular forces. As mentioned earlier, the regular forces were rarely permitted to accept battle in unfavorable situations, and were supposed to slip away when in danger of attack from superior French forces. These tactics were essentially like those of guerrillas, who strike and run and avoid battles at almost any cost. But unlike the guerrillas, who hit in order to cause confusion, destroy certain property, and keep the enemy off balance, the regular forces struck to annihilate.

THE OFFENSIVE

The Viets taught that there were four important prerequisites for a successful attack: the proper choice of time, a careful plan, adequate preparation, and high combative spirit.

Timing of the attack was obviously dependent on the time needed for planning and for concentrating the troops, as well as on the general situation. To a great extent, however, it also depended on the enemy. When the Viets decided to attack a post or fort, it was not just a matter of preparing a plan and then executing it. They would watch the garrison over a period of time in order to discover enemy habits and weaknesses. For instance, they would try to determine when the guards were changed, whether certain guards were habitually not alert, and at what times key officers or noncoms might be expected to be absent; and they would look for any signs of complacency or laxity among members of the garrison. All such intelligence information was then incorporated in the final plan, which specified time and locale of the main effort, points of secondary attacks, installations to be neutralized by firepower, and provisions for retreat. Each subordinate unit was assigned a specific job, and all details were worked out and discussed with the officers and noncoms. Sometimes the Vietminh would have a rehearsal of the attack, using specially constructed facsimiles of the French post or fort. All necessary equipment, arms, and ammunition having been procured, the Viets then set about explaining to the troops the reason for the attack and the importance of its success, rousing them to a high pitch of fanaticism and self-sacrifice, for a combat spirit equal to the task at hand was regarded as an indispensable element in the preparations.

The Viet units often moved to and from the battlefields by infiltration, which they practiced with great skill, thereby escaping air and ground detection and avoiding the danger of providing a target for air attack. They often infiltrated right through the French units so as to create greater surprise by attacking the enemy from both sides. The French have estimated that the Viets could infiltrate several individuals through a zone with a 1,300-yard perimeter, several platoons if the perimeter was 2,200 yards, and several companies where it was 4,400 yards long. If the perimeter was still longer, they might succeed in infiltrating a battalion and even a regiment. The Hanoi Delta perimeter, for example, with its posts about two-thirds of a mile apart, had virtually no protection against Vietminh infiltration.[1]

The Vietminh usually attacked at night, because this gave them several advantages over the French. Not only were the French considered poor night fighters, but in the darkness they lacked air support, and artillery support was difficult. A typical attack would begin at midnight or soon thereafter and break off at nine or ten in the morning. Whenever possible, the Viets would aim at complete surprise, often giving up preparatory fires to that end. The main effort, sometimes as much as nine-tenths of the attacking force, usually was concentrated on a very narrow front. The remainder made diversionary and noisy attacks, often before the main assault (especially if surprise was impossible to achieve), and their firepower would be directed at a few critical points.

Normally, four groups were involved in the attack. The first of these manned the heavy supporting weapons (usually automatic weapons, mortars, and recoilless rifles), whose aim was to neutralize one or two important enemy positions, such as the radio, the command post, or heavy weapons. If the attack were unsuccessful, their fire was to cover the retreat. The second group would be the assault engineers or dynamiters. These men, who might be a company or a platoon, ran forward or infiltrated the enemy lines and exploded dynamite in critical areas of the fort or post so as to create a breach. Leaving all personal weapons behind in their trenches, the dynamiters were armed only with explosives, which they sometimes carried on the ends of bamboo poles that could be forced into wire entanglements, and on occasion even tied to their own bodies in order to hurl themselves with the charges into enemy wire or walls. If they were able to return, they retrieved their weapons and assisted in the general attack. Once the enemy weapons had been neutralized and the dynamiters had created a breach, the third group—shock troops or assault infantry—moved forward, usually in three groups and on a narrow front, and attempted to overwhelm the post. The fourth was a reserve group, which covered the shock troops with fire, assisted in the attack, and either exploited the success or covered the retreat.

Although fighting in the attacked enemy positions was admittedly difficult, the Vietminh felt that it could be done successfully if four principles were observed: (1) Careful planning and training were essential. The planning was usually done with the aid of sand boards or other replicas of the French posts, and the attack was rehearsed many times. (2) In order to destroy the main enemy installations, the troops had to penetrate as deeply as possible and could not allow themselves to be kept out on the periphery of the fort. (3) There had to be close co-operation and co-ordination among the dynamiters, fire-support units, and shock troops. (4) A successful operation required close liaison between the attacking unit and its regiment and neighboring units.

The Vietminh were careful, also, to anticipate strong enemy reactions and counterattacks. Counterattacks, especially, were considered excellent opportunities to destroy an enemy who had left his shelter, and special plans were made for this contingency. On the other hand, Viet tactical doctrine demanded that if the Viets' own attacking troops were caught in three enemy fires, they concentrate on one and ignore the other two. Whenever they were themselves caught by a frontal attack, they were to avoid the strong places and counterattack the weak. When stopped by an artillery barrage, they were instructed either to retreat, dig in, and await artillery support, or if they were close to the enemy, to "cling" to him. When cut off or encircled, they were to try either to break through at one point or to disband and seek their way out individually.

The Vietminh believed (and their training instructions said so quite explicitly) that if the secret of an impending attack was well kept and the action instantaneous, even a handful of lightly equipped but well-armed assailants, under cover of night or expert camouflage, could sometimes smash a numerically superior enemy even in an attack on a post. This presupposed being informed to the hour and even to the minute of all activities in the post, so as to be able to profit from the moment when the enemy relaxed his watch in order to launch the attack.

CONTROLLING THE LINES OF COMMUNICATION

Much of the war effort on both sides was devoted to the battle for communications. The Vietminh tried to paralyze the French by denying them the use of roads, paths, and waterways. The greatest part of guerrilla activity was devoted to mining and destroying roads. In certain areas, the Vietminh regularly cut the roads at night and the French attempted to repair them during the day. Nearly everywhere, French soldiers had to check the roads for mines and cuts every morning before they could be used.

The ambush was the Vietminh's favorite means of attack on communications. This was not a spur-of-the-moment tactic but entailed considerable planning and preparation. Not only did guerrillas and regional troops ambush isolated French vehicles and units, but there were major ambushes of larger French formations. The Vietminh particularly liked to ambush relief units, using the following tactics: A stationary element, often composed of one company (which we shall call the "second element"), would straddle the road at a given point, where it could effectively block off any advance. Approximately 500 to 1,000 yards farther in the direction from which the relief column was coming, the "first element," composed of perhaps five units, was placed on both sides of the road. Finally, a "third element," about three companies strong and called the "rear ambush," waited at a distance of still another 1,000 yards behind the first element. Positions were carefully chosen and weapons artfully concealed. As the relieving force advanced down the road, it passed unhindered and unsuspecting by the third and first elements, but was stopped by the second element blocking the road. As soon as it was demobilized, the other two elements struck. The major element, in the middle, attacked the main force, while the third element, in the rear, attempted to cut off any retreat as well as possible relief forces.[2] The French have complained that, in spite of air and other observation means, they found it almost impossible to detect these ambushes and were nearly always trapped in them. The only defense against them was to devise means of reducing their effectiveness. Sometimes the French would make their columns longer than the stretch covered by the ambushing elements, thereby enabling part of their forces to escape and another part to come to the rescue of the trapped units. Also, they equipped the relief columns with artillery and armor to help rout the rebels. Then, too, they discovered that they could send a single vehicle, and even two or three vehicles, down the road without having them molested by the Vietminh, who were waiting for larger prey. During clearing operations, they tried to provide air cover, which, they hoped, would discover or discourage any ambush. Most of these measures, however, fell short of success, and the French lived in fear of ambushes to the end of the war.

THE DEFENSIVE

Following the precepts of Mao, "If the enemy attacks, I disappear; if he defends, I harass; and if he retreats, I attack," the Vietminh avoided defensive combat whenever possible. The fact that their few vital installations were in distant and difficult areas beyond the reach of French ground forces usually allowed them to refuse combat if they wished.

Vietminh units, no matter what positions they were in, had plans for retreat. A classic example of this tactic was furnished in August, 1948, on the Plaine des Joncs, a great swampy area in Cochinchina. The French had discovered the location of the command post of Nguyen Binh, the Viet commander of

Cochinchina, and mounted a land and air operation with the objective of seizing or killing him and his staff. Several battalions plowed through the mud, while more than two companies of paratroopers jumped right on the command post. Surprise was complete. A few shots were fired at the paratroopers as they descended and a short skirmish ensued as they landed, but almost immediately, at a given signal, all combat broke off. The Viet enemy just disappeared, and neither the surrounding French land forces nor the paratroopers could find any of the defenders. It was clear that the Vietminh had detailed plans for such an occasion and had executed them perfectly.

There were two possible methods for disappearing. One was to retreat into previously prepared hiding places in the area, such as subterranean caves, specially constructed holes, and positions prepared in the banks of rivers and originating below the water level. All such places were cleverly camouflaged, and only very few persons knew of their location. The other method was to retreat in small groups or individually, and either disappear into the woods or melt into the population of a neighboring village or city.

When the Vietminh did decide to defend a place, they proceeded by a very careful plan. Their techniques and tactics of defense were best illustrated in the villages. Having decided to defend a given village, they would work out a detailed program for its fortification and active defense. Individual shelter and hiding places, usually underground and connected by tunnels, were constructed in such a way that a defender could fire from one place, disappear, and then fire from another. Some of the individual holes were supplied with food and water, in case concealment was necessary for several days. They were so well camouflaged that the French often used dogs to sniff them out, and the Viets, in turn, had to use lime in the entrances to stop the dogs. Even good fields of fire often were sacrificed for the sake of better camouflage, and the defenders were allowed to disclose the location of their hiding places only to their leaders.

Villages in the Tonkin were already partially fortified against pirates and animals, and the Vietminh improved these existing defenses by adding anti-tank obstacles, mines, and other modern devices. During the first years of the war, they tried to make every village impregnable, but they soon realized that this was impossible, and restricted themselves to making it as difficult as possible for the enemy to advance into a village. Their first fortified villages all had identical defense plans, as the French soon found out. Thereafter, the Viet varied their plans for defense and thus complicated the attackers' problem.

A network of guards protected each such village and the sectors within it. During daylight hours the guards, disguised as peasants or workers, were placed at a half-mile to a mile from the village. Their positions were changed frequently, and a messenger, also in disguise, was always at hand to take news of an enemy advance to the village. At night the guards were pulled in closer to the village and posted near the gates. Each sector had its own guard system and an accepted warning signal. At all times strangers were watched and their credentials carefully checked. There were liaison channels to neighboring villages and higher headquarters.

The Viets made every effort to confuse the French as to the location of the defenders, and often enticed them into prepared traps, where they were then surrounded. When attacked, the village defenders were to hit at the enemy continuously as he approached, entered, and penetrated the village. It was not expected that the enemy would be annihilated in the initial phase. As soon as he weakened, however, a counterattack was launched with the aim of annihilation. If, on the other hand, the French continued to press forward, retreat would be ordered.

In the defense of villages, as in all situations, the Vietminh, reluctant to lose even irregular guerrillas, laid careful plans for retreat. In a hopeless fight, the defenders were instructed, upon a prearranged signal for disengagement, to retreat to their holes or abandon the villages by routes indicated in advance.

THE CASE OF DIEN BIEN PHU

The battle of Dien Bien Phu deserves special mention, as it was not typical of the fighting in Indochina. In the autumn of 1953, the French government determined that Laos should be defended and, almost simultaneously, negotiated a defense treaty with the Laotian government. The French commander in Indochina, General Henri Navarre, was instructed to defend Laos but not to endanger the safety of the Expeditionary Corps. Navarre knew he could not defend Laos by a war of movement or by any defensive line and decided that the only way was to establish a strategically located aero-ground strong point, which, he hoped, would prevent a massive invasion. Furthermore, there was some expectation that Giap's forces would thereby be drawn into a set battle with resulting heavy casualties for the Vietminh. He recognized, however, that such a strong point would not prevent all enemy military movements into Laos.

The village of Dien Bien Phu—located in a valley roughly ten by five miles and more than two hundred miles from the French air bases in Hanoi and Vientiane—was selected as the site for this strong point and was occupied late in November, 1953. Although Navarre recognized that this was not the ideal site for such an operation, he considered it the best in the area. He was criticized at the time for selecting Dien Bien Phu, and has been since, for this meant that the enemy would occupy all the surrounding high ground. French air force officers have also stated that had they been consulted, the position would not have been agreed to, as it was at the extreme range of the fighter aircraft which were to support the base. The controversy over these points continued even after the war and can never really be resolved, though—with the wisdom of hindsight—Navarre's critics may be said to have been correct in their assessment of the position.

The French seriously underestimated the artillery available to the Vietminh and the method in which it would be employed. The Chinese had provided Giap with far more regular artillery than French intelligence knew. But the most significant development was that the Vietminh used their artillery in direct fire, and not indirectly, as the French—and for that matter American—artillerymen had predicted. Instead of positioning behind the hills, which would have put the French forts out of range, the Vietminh moved their guns at night onto the forward slopes of the hills. There they carefully dug in and camouflaged single pieces, which were fired point-blank at the French, and with devastating effect. Using this tactic, the Vietminh soon knocked out or neutralized the French artillery and thus were able to creep closer to the French forts and launch massive attacks. With the French artillery out of commission, the Vietminh were then able to bring their own antiaircraft guns much closer to the forts and thus make air resupply very difficult and dangerous. Indeed, by April, only parachute drops were possible, and those at successively higher altitudes. The French fighter aircraft, which could remain in the area for only a short time because of range limitations, had to be used mainly for flank suppression instead of close support.

A second major miscalculation of the French was that Giap would not engage in a siege operation. But this is exactly what he did in fact undertake. A special road was constructed to the Dien Bien Phu area, so that supplies could be brought directly from China; and, beginning in December and January, supplies and ammunition were stocked for a long siege. The French-led mountain tribes that were to sabotage the Vietminh supply routes failed completely in this mission. As the Vietminh artillery smashed the French artillery and defenses, Giap pushed forward a complex system of trenches and dugouts. French aerial photography of the area in February and March revealed a mass of trenches that tightened increasingly around the beleaguered forts in the manner of a true eighteenth-century siege.

In March, after artillery supremacy had been largely gained and supplies assembled, Giap launched the first of his massive attacks on Dien Bien Phu. Gabrielle and Beatrice, the two outposts on the high ground within the valley, were the first to fall under the waves of Giap's massed infantry. The loss of these forts confirmed to the defenders that Giap had in fact gained full artillery supremacy and that they could not effectively reply to his fire.

In May, the Vietminh launched the attack that finally overran the position, and on May 8, the last French troops surrendered. Thus the battle of Dien Bien Phu was over and Giap had won a decisive victory.

French casualties, including prisoners, totaled about 12,000 men, which was only about 6 per cent of the total expeditionary force. Giap's casualties were numerically probably twice those of the French. Though the loss of Dien Bien Phu and its garrison was a bitter and unexpected defeat for France and a blow to Western strength, it was not in the military sense a decisive one. Its main impact was in the political arena, where it was sufficient to persuade the French to negotiate and end the war.

NOTES

1. However, French artillery, with massed preplanned fire, was able to interfere with attacks and large-scale attempts at penetration.

2. Obviously not every Viet ambush followed this pattern to the letter. This illustration is provided chiefly to show the care and planning that went into a typical ambush.

Chapter 5

VIETMINH REACTIONS TO FRENCH TACTICS AND AIR POWER

Particularly important in a study of this nature are the responses of each side to new tactics and techniques of the other. The present chapter will deal primarily with Vietminh reactions to French innovations, but it will examine also some of the ways in which the French responded to the tactics and countertactics of the Vietminh.

UNDERMINING THE POLICY OF PACIFICATION

Until 1950, the major effort of the French was in the south, in Cochinchina, the region of their greatest successes. Here the French had adopted a policy of pacification, with the threefold aim of crushing rebel bands, helping the local people establish defenses of their own, and restoring normal life to the villages and cities. Pacification thus had both a military and a political aspect. While there was considerable military success, the French tended to fall short on the political side. Their reluctance to grant independence to Vietnam and their frequent failure to follow up military successes by re-establishing regular administration and services in the pacified regions prevented their victories from being clear-cut and permanent.

From a military point of view, pacification actions were mainly of two types: sweeping operations, to clear an area between two or more points held by the French; and extending operations, to spread French control further out into Vietminh territory. The pacification forces, which varied in size from a few companies to several battalions, were made up primarily of infantry, but included also engineers, artillerymen, and tanks. They usually operated in columns, as the nature of their equipment and armament forced them to stick to such primary means of communication as roads or dikes. This requirement not only exposed them to certain Vietminh tactics but limited the effectiveness of their actions. Occasionally, the French engaged in sweeping operations in which the infantry would comb the countryside. However, in swampy terrain and mountainous or forested regions, this was exceedingly slow and difficult, and the enemy usually escaped. Quite often, the French tried first to cut off all means of escape by encirclement and then to sweep the enclosed area, but the Viets' skill at infiltration frequently foiled these efforts.

Certain other factors contributed to making these operations less successful than they might have been. French intelligence was poor and most Vietminh areas seemed to have forewarning of the enemy's coming. The French soldiers frequently conducted themselves in a manner that alienated the native population, and did not seem to realize the importance of winning the local people to their side through positive acts. As already pointed out, inadequate political follow-up of military victory slowed down the return to normal administrative life in villages and towns in which French control had been re-established. The French also were a long time developing an adequate psychological program for either the civilians or the military. Finally, the difficult terrain and debilitating weather proved a serious hindrance to the French advance.

Nevertheless, pacification made considerable headway in the south, particularly before 1950. Recognizing it as a threat, the Vietminh devised tactics to undermine it. First and most important was the political counteraction. Viet agents would infiltrate a village or an area and establish a cell, which became the center for counterpacification, spreading propaganda and recruiting adherents to the Vietminh cause among the population. Having once gained a foothold and won some support for the struggle against the French, the Vietminh would proceed more aggressively. They often attacked and killed natives who attempted to co-operate with the French or to oppose Vietminh penetration. These examples succeeded in terrifying the local people and proved a strong deterrent to pro-French activity in the area.

PUTTING THE FRENCH ON THE DEFENSIVE

On the military side, the Vietminh improved defenses or fortified the villages so as to make French clearing operations more difficult. Also, since they especially feared the French encircling actions, they issued detailed instructions on counterencirclement tactics. On the major points, these followed the general tactical rules that Viet combatants must try to avoid any conflict not in their favor or, if caught in a tight encirclement, must concentrate on the weak point of the encircling forces and fight their way through. The manuals stressed again and again that encircling forces were never strong at all points and that a determined attack could always effect a break. If in danger of being encircled by a particularly strong French force on easy terrain, the Viet units were urged to withdraw from the area in time and leave no one for the French to capture.

Developments in the Tonkin area in the north were a particularly good example of Viet military countertactics that succeeded in forcing the enemy from the offensive into a defensive posture. While the French had occupied certain border positions in order to cut the Vietminh off from Chinese aid, their primary aim was to create a strong-hold in the Red River Delta region that would not only serve as a secure operational base but would also enable them to cut off the Viet food supply and thus force the Vietminh to fight for it in the Delta. To this end, General de Lattre attempted to form a front, in the Western sense, composed of forts and posts, the smallest of which were only about half a mile apart, while the larger "mother" forts were spaced at several miles from one another. The forts ranged from simple towers, surrounded by barbed wire and held by a few dozen men, to elaborate fortifications with heavy arms and garrisoned by several hundred men. However, the French recognized that static defenses alone were rarely successful, and, further- more, De Lattre had no intention of assuming a defensive posture. Once the base had been made secure, fortifications properly provided, and the forces redeployed, so-called "mobile groups," composed of infantry, armor, and artil- lery and representing the cream of the French troops, were to be used as offen- sive striking forces to attack key Vietminh installations and force combat on their own terms. This strategy, however, was foiled by a series of Viet tactics, which succeeded in tying up so many French troops that only few offensive actions could be undertaken, and the French posture remained essentially defensive.

After their surprising victory on the border posts in 1950, the Vietminh at first had continued to launch major attacks around the edges of the Red River Delta but had given up when they suffered heavy casualties. Thereafter, they infiltrated large units, up to division size, through the French posts and forts to assist their guerrillas within the Delta. It was said that the French held the Delta in the daytime and the Vietminh held it at night. Even within this center of the French defenses, the Viets used mines and ambushes, and destroyed portions of roads, in order to disrupt French civilian and military traffic. There was excellent co-ordination between the clandestine activities inside and the operations of the Vietminh forces outside the Delta, as resistance activity within was intensified whenever the French struck at the Vietminh outside. It has been reliably estimated that in 1953 about 35,000 Vietminh were tying up three times their number of French forces in the Delta. As in the counterpaci- fication effort in the south, the Viets made examples of individuals in order to frighten any natives who might want to support the French. They also attacked many of the posts or forts, particularly the more isolated ones. These were usually surprise night attacks, which had been carefully planned, with high superiority in manpower. After the arrival of Chinese aid, and with it some heavier guns, the Viets were able to use armor-piercing shells against the forts, many of which were old and somewhat flimsily constructed and could not stand up against this type of action.

The French, of course, did not accept these countertactics passively. They brought in dogs from France, which they used to detect the approach of any enemy, particularly during the night, but the dogs were often unable to distinguish between friend and foe. On a very limited scale, the French attempted to reduce the difficulties of night combat by illuminating the area after dark, but their supply of equipment was inadequate for this purpose. Then, also, they constructed their newer forts underground, with just a few observation points above ground. This did indeed make attacks more difficult and the use of armor-piercing shells less effective, but most forts, unless relieved by mobile columns, fell before a determined Vietminh attack.

In the course of the war, as the Vietminh developed their offensive power, including units large enough to undertake major operations, the French were put more and more on the defensive, and were forced to find ways of countering certain Vietminh tactics and techniques by developing new techniques of their own. One of their most important innovations was to create what they called "air-ground strong points" in the mountain areas controlled by the Vietminh but inhabited by people generally sympathetic to the French. Since the French needed to keep some troops and strong points in these areas, and their land communications were extremely unreliable, they put individual garrisons in the vicinity of their airstrips and supplied them by air. With these strong points as bases, and sometimes with paratroop support, they were able to beat off many Vietminh attacks and maintain the French "presence." However, the small number of available cargo planes and the great need for French troops in the Delta limited the number of troops that could be used in strong points, as was shown, of course, at Dien Bien Phu.

A second countertechnique, based on the experience gained in France during World War II, was to form partisan groups in the mountainous areas to act as a maquis against the Vietminh. During the battle of Dien Bien Phu, the French claim to have had in the area the equivalent of about fifteen battalions of partisan guerrillas who were to have interfered with Vietminh supply lines. The action remained very limited, and most French officers were disappointed at the results. But it is true that on several occasions the Vietminh had to detach regiments to clean out areas where the French had penetrated with their guerrillas.

NEUTRALIZATION OF AIR POWER

Throughout the war, the Vietminh admitted that one of the greatest advantages of the French was that of air power and, indeed, of absolute air superiority. Having acknowledged this, however, they explained in numerous manuals and propaganda pamphlets how this French advantage could be neutralized. Before examining how they went about minimizing the effects of French air power, it is well to look briefly at the kind of air power the French had in Indochina, the manner in which they employed it, and the difficulties of operation under which they labored. While published statistics are inexact, the following seems to be a fairly accurate estimate of French aircraft in Indochina: In November, 1951, there were 158 fighters, 42 light bombers, 75 transports, 28 reconnaissance planes, and 105 light aircraft. Two years later, in November, 1953, the French had 120 fighters, 42 light bombers, 84 transports, 16 reconnaissance craft, and approximately 237 other planes, including light craft and trainers. In March, 1954, at the beginning of the battle of Dien Bien Phu, there were 123 fighters plus 40 carrier-borne fighters, 41 light bombers, 124 transports, 16 reconnaissance planes, and 230 other aircraft.[1] These figures did not include some hired civilian cargo planes, which helped with air supply.

The French air force in Indochina operated under severe difficulties. In the first place, there were only about five first-class airfields, which, for some time at least, put a ceiling on the number of aircraft that could be operated in this theater. Constructing new airfields was a slow and difficult process. In the delta regions, it was said to take one ton of crushed rock for every square yard of runway, and this rock had to be allowed to settle slowly. As a result, even under a "crash" program, airfields could not safely be constructed quickly. The mountain areas were generally in Vietminh hands and, besides, presented construction problems of their own. The second major difficulty in planning for French air operations was that the weather was bad much of the year and varied greatly from one part of Indochina to another. There were few weather stations, and even if the weather was good at Hanoi, it might not be good over the target or between target and take-off point. Thirdly, the French air force complained that their maps were unreliable. Heights of peaks and other essential terrain information were inaccurate, and in certain areas, therefore, planes could not operate safely. And last of all, radio guidance and navigational aids were inadequate for normal flying, and still more so for night and bad-weather operations.

French air force officers were almost unanimous in their criticism of the command structure. Serving under an army commander in chief who was responsible for the entire Indochina theater, they felt that they were rarely involved in the planning and that had they been consulted, many operations would have been carried out differently and more effectively. They believed that, in general, air power was misused. One of their complaints was that it was tied too much to the army; it was, for example, often used for direct support when it could more properly have been employed for interdiction and other air targets.

Since the Vietminh did not have any air force, the battle for air superiority never came into play; to the end of the war, the French were able to use their limited air power in a variety of ways, including interdiction, direct support of the army, air supply, and the launching of airborne operations.

Vietminh antiaircraft capability improved in the course of the war, especially after the advent of Chinese aid. During the siege of Dien Bien Phu, as we have seen, the Viets were able to knock down a number of French planes and to keep most of the others at altitudes too high for effective assistance and accurate supply drops to the troops. Though apparently antiaircraft guns were not radar-controlled, there were some excellent Russian pieces that were skillfully used. Even before they acquired antiaircraft, however, the Vietminh had managed to shoot down quite a few planes simply with rifles and machine guns, and guerrillas had tried to incapacitate planes on the ground. It is interesting to note that the Vietminh attacked chiefly the transport planes and rarely molested the fighters.

While the French had made sporadic interdiction efforts all along, it was not until 1952 that they really planned an extensive interdiction program against the Vietminh's supply routes, particularly those leading from the Chinese border. In this campaign, they concentrated on two types of targets: truck garages and warehouses where supplies might be stored, and difficult stretches of road that were hard to bypass. Most of their targets were within the Lang Son–Bac Kan–Cao Bang triangle. The French air force made much of the success of this offensive and, at one time, claimed to have reduced the flow of Chinese aid from 1,500 to 250 tons a month. The Vietminh reacted to this intensified interdiction effort in several ways, none of them particularly novel. In the first place, as most transportation took place at night and the French had practically no night capability, the coolies remained relatively safe then. If the tactical situation on the battlefield made it necessary to move during daylight hours, coolies tried, whenever possible, to employ unknown paths and new routes. This made the French air effort more difficult, since small paths with coolie columns were very hard to spot, and the French reconnaissance capability had declined by 1952. At critical points on the roads, the Vietminh sometimes stationed repair crews that would rebuild any bridges that were destroyed. At other times, they merely used boats to move the supplies across.

Direct air support for the French ground forces was used to a considerable extent. Many of the French themselves have felt that this was a mistake in view of its admittedly limited value. Except in battle, the Vietminh units were extremely difficult to locate, as they were usually well dug in and were very artful when it came to dispersal, camouflage, and concealment. Also, they would often mingle with the populace, and the French air force either could not distinguish them from the civilians or, if it could, was unable to strike at them for fear of hitting some of the village or city people. Vietminh attacks, as stated earlier, always began at night, when the French air force had very limited capability. If the battle continued into the daylight hours, an effective method by which the Viets avoided air attack was to "cling" to the enemy, that is, to stay so close to the French forces that air fire would hit both friend and foe.

In the final stage of the war, air supply of the French garrisons became increasingly important and lacked only an adequate number of transport aircraft to have been still more effective. The French advantage in air supply went virtually unchallenged in view of the opponent's limited antiaircraft capability. The Vietminh made every effort to infiltrate agents into French air bases, and even the most heavily guarded planes were found sabotaged. During the battle of Dien Bien Phu, when air supply was keeping the French garrison going, the Vietminh, in a noteworthy example of co-ordination in their war effort, conducted a special sabotage campaign in the Delta to destroy these cargo planes. It was indicative of the importance they attached to the air supply capability of the French.

Though airborne operations were important in Indochina, the limited French airlift capability precluded large operations. Usually only one battalion, and even in the latter stages of the war never more than two or three battalions, could be airlifted for a single operation. Despite this, the French rarely achieved surprise, for their reconnaissance planes surveying the area prior to attack, and the advance of French ground units toward a given area, would often alert the Vietminh to a possible airborne attack. Also, the very nature of the war made paratroop operations less effective than they would have been in a conventional war. As there was no front, there was nobody to cut off, and paratroopers therefore were usually employed against a key point with the hope of destroying it. In most cases, a battalion proved too small to do the job, particularly during the latter phases of the war, when the Vietminh units were large. Occasional plans to have the paratroopers link up with the ground forces usually produced disappointing results.

Nevertheless, the Vietminh feared airborne operations and took precautions against them. All of their units, fortified villages, and other important areas posted guards whose mission it was to look out for aircraft, and particularly paratroopers. In certain spots that seemed especially suitable for landings, the Vietminh put up pointed bamboo sticks on which the paratroopers would impale themselves. Then again, if threatened by paratroop attack, the Viets would just disappear and leave no one for the paratroopers to fight. And lastly, the French were compelled to gather up their chutes after every jump, and one-fourth to one-third of the jumping unit would be tied up in this task, often for half a day, reducing the number of effectives who were free to fight. The Vietminh took advantage of this opportunity to attack the chute collectors and thus make the landing more difficult and costly in lives.

***

As in all wars, there was thus a constant interplay between the combatants: Each devised new tactics and strategies and the other attempted to foil them.

The Vietminh were seldom slow to spot a new French tactic and to issue instructions on how to counter it. The French were somewhat less flexible and tended to adhere to their accustomed methods of warfare even when these were no longer effective. The renewal of the war several years later involved again the interaction of two quite different opponents. The subsequent introduction of major U.S. elements made the interplay even more interesting and important.

NOTE

1. General L. M. Chassin, *Aviation Indochine (Air Power in Indochina)* (Amiot-Dumont: Paris, 1954).

Chapter 6

THE RISE OF THE VIET CONG

The military struggle between the Vietminh and the French was terminated in July, 1954. It was hoped at the Geneva Conference that the geographical division of Vietnam would be temporary and the cessation of fighting permanent, but the reverse has turned out to be the case. Fighting was resumed in the late 1950's and gradually increased in intensity and scale through the 1960's to the present bitter war of 1967, while the demarcation line has become fixed and the two zones go their separate ways.

The Agreements on the Cessation of Hostilities (July 20, 1954) and the Final Declaration of the Geneva Conference (July 21, 1954)—or the Geneva Accords, as they are generally known—officially ended the fighting in Vietnam and attempted to establish a *modus vivendi* until a political settlement could be arranged.[1] The cease-fire agreements were basically military in scope. A provisional military demarcation line, with a five-kilometer demilitarized zone on both sides, was established roughly along the 17th parallel, thus dividing Vietnam into two separate zones. The military forces of the two parties were to be regrouped in their appropriate zones within 300 days. Both parties were enjoined not to undertake "reprisals or discriminations against persons or organizations on account of their activities during the hostilities." The agreements banned the reinforcement of forces, the introduction of more modern arms and equipment, and the establishment of foreign bases in either zone. Also created under the agreements was an International Commission, composed of India, Canada, and Poland, for the "control and supervision over the application of the provisions of the agreement." The cease-fire agreements were signed by military officers from France (for the South) and the Communist Democratic Republic of Vietnam (for the North); France and the D.R.V.N.

were thus responsible for enforcing the cease-fire in their respective zones. The agreements were not signed by representatives of either the Government of South Vietnam (G.V.N.) or the United States.

The Final Declaration of the Conference, signed by no nation, noted and endorsed the main provisions of the cease-fire. While the cease-fire agreements more or less assumed that there would be an election for the unification of Vietnam, the Final Declaration, being more politically inclined, was quite specific. It called for a future political settlement and a general election with a secret ballot to be held in July, 1956—thus allowing two years to re-establish some order in the two zones. It also specifically provided that each person should be free to decide in which zone he would live. The participants in the conference agreed to respect the sovereignty of Laos, Cambodia, and Vietnam—thus recognizing the supposedly temporary nature of the division of Vietnam—and to refrain from interfering in their internal affairs. They also agreed to consult on any questions referred to them by the International Control Commission.[2]

The D.R.V.N. had some reason to be dissatisfied with this settlement and felt that the Soviet Union and China had pressed it to agree to terms less favorable than it deserved. Although the military significance of the defeat at Dien Bien Phu can be exaggerated, it is true that the Vietminh were slowly chewing up the French military forces in Vietnam. Even more important, the continuing casualties and the apparently unending nature of the struggle had convinced Paris that the conflict must end. Given this situation, the D.R.V.N. considered that it had received less territory than it should have, had given more generous overall terms to the French than they deserved, and had accepted, at least temporarily, the division of its country. The D.R.V.N. leaders also recognized that the implementation of the agreements depended to a large extent on the willingness and capability of the French. If France somehow failed, the promise of Geneva would be lost. They thus felt partially cheated of the victory they had won, and they were concerned about the eventual enforcement of the settlement.

However, the provision for elections in July, 1956, gave Hanoi hope of achieving a united Vietnam under its leadership. It was most probably this expectation that led the D.R.V.N. to sign the agreements. In 1954, it seemed clear to most observers, as well as to Hanoi, that such elections would be won by Ho Chi Minh's regime. A second and even more immediate possibility was that the Saigon regime would never consolidate its position and might even collapse before the elections, thus giving Hanoi victory by default. In such a situation there might be no need for an election except to confirm and legalize the takeover.

THE SITUATION AFTER GENEVA

In mid-1954, South Vietnam was indeed in disarray, and the likelihood that an effective government could be established did not seem great. Bao Dai, the

Chief of State and former Emperor, did not possess the confidence of the people and was having trouble finding a leader to form a government. On June 4, while the Geneva Conference was still in session, Bao Dai appointed Ngo Dinh Diem, a long-time nationalist who had been absent from the country for several years, as Premier of the Government of South Vietnam. As yet, there existed practically no governmental apparatus, and Diem did not control all of the Saigon-Cholon area, much less the countryside. Few observers expected him to survive many months, and almost no one gave him much chance of restoring order and creating an operational government in the South. However, within a year, Diem managed to defeat the paramilitary forces of the politico-religious sects (Hoa Hao, Cao Dai, and Binh Xuyen) and drive their remnants underground, to build an army and some civil administration, and to begin to extend the control of the central government into the countryside. The United States offered support, advice, and economic aid to the new Premier. Diem's successes gained him some support and popularity within his own country and a certain respect from other countries. Through a popular referendum he was able to oust Bao Dai as Chief of State and proclaim the Republic of Vietnam. The French withdrew their Expeditionary Corps and dissolved their High Command ahead of schedule; thus one of the signatories of the Geneva Accords was no longer on the scene. Given his surprisingly strong base at home, Diem announced in 1955 that he would not agree to elections as provided for by the Geneva agreements. Thus, as 1956 approached, it seemed unlikely that the Saigon government would collapse and even more unlikely that the elections would be held.

At the same time, it seemed clear from the statements and actions of the leaders of the D.R.V.N. that they had not given up their intention to unify Vietnam under their rule. Early in 1955, Ho Chi Minh called for continued effort in both the North and South for unification and final victory, and in September, 1955, he created the Fatherland Front of Vietnam, whose program was clearly directed at unification. Some of the Vietminh who remained in the South and were later captured have said they were instructed by the Fatherland Front to support the Geneva Accords in general and specifically the elections as the surest way to unification. There seems to have been some pressure on Hanoi from the Soviet Union and China (who for different reasons did not wish to disturb the international scene) to abide by the Geneva Accords and to wait for the elections, which almost everyone thought Hanoi would win. The Vietminh may also have been weak in the South immediately after the withdrawal of so many troops and adherents to the North. In late 1955, Hanoi appeared to be concentrating on consolidation of its regime in the North and striving for socialism and extensive social change through its drastic land reform, meanwhile hoping that the election would solve the unification problem in the South. But Hanoi had also made some plans for action in the South if the elections did not materialize.

In 1954, the Communists had taken North with them a number of troops and some carefully selected Southern adherents—perhaps a total of 80,000 to 100,000. (These are usually referred to as regroupees.) This action was in accordance with the provisions of the Geneva Agreements. Hanoi may also have wished to maintain as large an army as possible, and may have been planning to use these forces in the South at a later date. They represented a good basis for a "unified" Vietnamese Army and a potential Southern governmental cadre if elections were won by Ho Chi Minh's regime. If there were no elections, the regroupees could be used as a subversive cadre for future activity in the South. Hanoi had left 5,000 to 10,000 elite cadres and caches of weapons and supplies in the South. These cadres, who were mostly political and administrative personnel, blended into the countryside and did not begin their subversive operations until after July, 1956. The Vietminh also maintained some bases—notably in Quang Ngai and Binh Dinh provinces, in the mountains behind Nha Trang, in the northern portion of Tay Ninh Province, in Zone D, in certain areas of Kien Phong and An Xuyen provinces, and in the highlands, which they never ceased to administer and which Diem never penetrated—but they took few aggressive actions in 1954–56. However, when Hanoi wished to recommence its subversive activities in the South, local cadres and a skeletal administrative structure were available, and the regroupees represented potential reinforcements.

The elections were not held in 1956. The D.R.V.N. complained to the International Control Commission, and the Commission in turn complained to the co-chairmen of the Geneva Conference (Great Britain and the Soviet Union), but no action was taken. In November, 1956, as a result of long smoldering hostility toward the regime caused by the so-called land reform, uprisings occurred in the North and were brutally suppressed. Consequently, Hanoi was hardly in a good position to press for free elections. One might even speculate that Hanoi did not want elections at that time because of the unrest in the North and Diem's surprising strength in the South. In any case, the date for the elections passed without great demonstrations within Vietnam or significant protest from any other country. Thus the provisional agreement made in 1954 took on more aspects of permanence. But the promise of elections apparently had been an important factor in persuading Hanoi to accept the Geneva Accords, and the failure to hold them gave Hanoi an excuse for seeking other means of unification—and the chance to capitalize on unsettling developments in the South.

Ngo Dinh Diem, in attempting to form a strong, largely dictatorial government, not unnaturally alienated many groups of people. Local officials, often arrogant and inefficient, created or aggravated hostility toward the Saigon regime. The majority of the members of the politico-religious sects opposed Diem after his defeat of their armies; they wished to strike back in any way they could. The sects were in no position to overthrow Diem and regain their special privileges—their apparent goal—but by cooperating with other groups they could harass and weaken his regime. Other groups, nationalists and dissidents, who were allowed no part in Diem's government and were increasingly likely to be persecuted, saw two alternatives: to join the rebels or to flee the country. They shared the bitterness of the sect members but differed in their ultimate goals: They wanted a role in the government, not special group privileges. Some members of the Vietminh remained staunch revolutionaries, while many others lost interest and settled down as peaceful citizens, but all were persecuted and driven into the opposition by Diem's repressive measures. The Communists were certainly a danger, but the Saigon government had created unnecessarily fertile ground for a rebellion in the South by late 1956.

However, not all of this fertile ground was created by Diem's sometimes exaggerated repressive measures and police force. In its entire history, Vietnam has only been united for a few years. It is a developing country and has never been a nation-state in the Western sense. There are historically divisive forces still at work. The loyalty of the people is often to a specific area, such as the Hué area, or to one of the regions of Vietnam—Cochinchina, Annam, or Tonkin—rather than to the nation as a whole. There is a strong tradition of village autonomy. There are also unassimilated minorities such as the Chinese, the *montagnards,* and the Khmers, who together represent about 10 to 15 per cent of the overall population and are very numerous in some portions of the country. The Catholic minority has created another force for division, and the Buddhists themselves are not a homogeneous group.

The Hoa Hao and the eclectic politico-religious sect the Cao Dai—both offsprings of the Buddhists—further complicate the problem. Secret societies (still unknown quantities) and parties—the Dai Viets and the VNQDD, among others—have their own ambitions and create friction within the country.[3] All these factors work against a strong, united Vietnam.

BEGINNINGS OF INSURGENCY

In the second half of 1956, there seemed to be the first definite indications of insurgent activity in the rural areas. There were subversive propaganda efforts, some terrorist raids, and the murder of a few officials. Some have argued that the responsibility for these acts lay with the remnants of the sects; others have held that the perpetrators were impatient Communists, frustrated by Geneva; still others have contended that the Communist cadres would hardly have undertaken such actions without the command, much less the permission of Hanoi.[4] The Diem regime held the third view and produced many captured documents that demonstrated Communist leadership of the subversion. Bernard Fall, hardly a Diem supporter, made a careful correlation between the areas where Communists were alleged by Saigon to have begun subversion and the areas where Hanoi complained to the International Control Commission of persecution against the Vietminh, and he demonstrated that they were largely the same. The information provided by Hanoi, he reasoned, was such that it must have come from an agent in the South, and he was led to the "inescapable" conclusion that there was some coordination between the North and the Southern insurgents.[5]

Viet Cong prisoners interrogated recently indicate that these early years (1956–59) were spent in spreading propaganda that stressed the colonial (American) and corrupt nature of the Diem government, and in working to reorganize the Vietminh and develop an insurgent structure. In their efforts to recruit new members, the Vietminh penetrated and gained some support from remnants of the sects. Their operations—illegal since they did not support the Geneva Accords but advocated overthrow of the government—were made difficult and dangerous by Diem's repressive campaign against all Vietminh and their families, whether they were active or not.

On the other hand, Diem was having trouble extending his power to the countryside and re-establishing the authority of government. He was not able to provide social services and opportunities for the rural population—a point constantly pressed by the Vietminh.

By late 1957, the insurgents were making their presence known. The newspapers carried an increasing and alarming number of stories of terrorist activities in the countryside. At the end of that year, the newspaper *Tu Do* maintained that "the security question in the provinces must be given top priority." At the same time, small numbers of peasants began leaving their farms because of insecurity. One observer has even claimed that "the cream of village officialdom" had been murdered as early as 1957.[6] Assassinations, kidnapings, and attacks on officials increased in 1958.[7] No one knows the exact number of casualties, as whatever records existed were inexact. One reliable estimate is that in 1957–60 some 2,000 officials were kidnaped and about 1,700 assassinated.[8] This is a staggering total for a nation of perhaps 14 million people trying to recover from war and move into the twentieth century.

The reviving Communist apparatus led this terror campaign designed to destroy the G.V.N., to gain control in the South, and to achieve unification with the North, but it gladly—if temporarily and cynically—accepted support from other dissidents, some of whom have been mentioned above.[9]

Most of the insurgents referred to themselves as Vietminh or members of The Resistance during this early period. After the formation of the National Liberation Front in late 1960, many, but by no means all, insurgents called themselves members of the Front. Others referred to the insurgent organization as the Party. In 1956, the Saigon government began to call the insurgents Viet Cong (Vietnamese Communist); this term became common usage by 1958 and has remained so to the present day.

While the sect members and other rebels considered the terror campaign primarily as a means of harassing the Saigon government, the Communists made much more careful and precise use of terror as one tool in their drive for total power. The campaign against lower officials was designed to discredit the Diem government by showing that it could not protect its own officials and to disable the government by killing or driving away its officials and replacing them with Communist personnel. These actions helped the Viet Cong gradually to expand their bases and war zones. Viet Cong attacks were almost always accompanied or followed by a propaganda team which explained why the official had been killed, how evil and corrupt the Diem government was, and how the rebels intended to improve the lot of the peasant. If the official was a bad one, the rebels took credit for ridding the people of an oppressor; if he was a good one, they said he was misguided and worked for the evil Diem. The success of the attacks had the additional effect of convincing the peasants of the strength of the rebels and encouraging their support.

The combination of skillful propaganda and terror with great organizational ability gave strength to the Viet Cong movement. In these early days of the insurgency, the Viet Cong were able to capitalize on the popularity of the Vietminh and to organize the agitprop teams developed so skillfully by General Giap in the earlier war. Their technique was to nurture latent grievances and dislike of Saigon into active hostility and hatred against the Diem regime. The proselytizing of the G.V.N. armed forces as well as the civilian officials was one of the most effective and demoralizing weapons wielded by the Viet Cong. This program *(binh van)* was directed particularly at the armed forces (ARVN) with the objective of incapacitating the army as the main support of the government. There was more emphasis on winning the people by sympathizing with their local grievances and advocating an end to the "oppressive and corrupt" Diem regime than on terrorizing them. Terror and coercive measures were reserved largely for the officials of the government, social workers and teachers, or other key persons who opposed or refused to cooperate with the Viet Cong—but the lesson was not lost on the population.

Beginning in 1958, Viet Cong guerrilla units were formed and trained for larger actions than assassinations and kidnapings. This development was natural in the evolution of the Communist insurgency. It made possible direct attacks on villages, small government outposts, and the *agrovilles*,[10] as well as small ambushes on the highways, railroads, and canals. These larger attacks were not only destructive, but had the even more important consequences of further discrediting and undermining the Saigon government and demonstrating the ever-increasing power and authority of the Viet Cong, who had begun to isolate the countryside from Saigon both physically and in a psychological sense. Since the Saigon government had always been strongly urban-oriented and lacked a real understanding and appreciation of the problems in the rural areas, this Communist strategy was bound to aggravate an already serious problem. For the same reason, inadequate attention was given the unrest and rising terror in the countryside.

The nature of the group that was able to organize skillfully and clandestinely, expand its political action, increase its terrorist activities, and launch these guerrilla attacks up until 1960 is not yet well known.[11] Some sources contend there was no central organization before the creation of the National Liberation Front (NLF) in 1960 and the People's Revolutionary Party in 1962 (see below). Emphasizing the variety and spontaneity of the opposition to Diem, they claim that there were only voluntary groupings that made sporadic attacks against the Diem regime.[12] This argument provides a necessary basis for the formation of the National Liberation Front—to fill the need for co-ordination. But there is much circumstantial and documentary evidence that even before the creation of the NLF there was one dominating and coordinating organization, composed of Vietminh cadres, most of whom were members of the Lao Dong Party, who had been left in the South and had blended into the rural areas and worked for the election until 1956. These cadres received some instructions and guidance from the North, and beginning in 1959 or even earlier, Hanoi began to order a few of the regroupees back to the South. They infiltrated along carefully prepared routes and returned to their original localities—often their own villages—where they began to organize or strengthen an opposition movement. Regroupees captured late in the war have told of their training in the North, their carefully planned trip South, and their instructions to intensify the struggle. The Communists systematically, but with difficulty in the face of Diem's repressive measures, revived and expanded the old Vietminh and developed an increasingly powerful insurgent apparatus.

FORMAL ORGANIZATION FOR INSURGENCY

It has been reported that in late 1958 Hanoi was dissatisfied with the development of the organization and the progress of the revolution. (It should be noted that the South had never reached the same level of participation as the North in the earlier "war of liberation" with the French.) In any case, Hanoi sent Le Duan, Secretary General of the Lao Dong Party, to the South during the winter of 1958–59 to gain firsthand information and to make specific recommendations. On his return to Hanoi in early 1959, Le Duan made a number of recommendations that led to actions in both the North and the South. In May, 1959, the Lao Dong Party Central Committee, meeting in Hanoi, stated that the time had come to smash the Diem government.[13] Le Duan himself announced at the Third National Congress of the Party in September, 1960, that the meeting would define the line for carrying out the socialist revolution in the North and the national revolution in the South, or the struggle for complete unification of the country and the overthrow of "the semifeudal, semicolonial Diem regime." He called for the creation of a successor to the Fatherland Front in the South. Shortly afterward, the Lao Dong Party circulated a draft outlining the structure and responsibilities of a new organization to be called the National Liberation Front. Finally, in January, 1961, Radio Hanoi broadcast the news that the NLF had been formed on December 20, 1960. This sequence of events may suggest that Le Duan was sent South not because of dissatisfaction with progress, but to make sure that the organization was really ready for the next phase of insurgency. Hanoi's statements that the time had come to crush Diem, and its organization of a mass front to lead the insurgency, indicate that the Communist Party leadership in the North believed that the organization in the South was probably in excellent shape and ready to create and manipulate the NLF and the whole revolution. Since the guerrilla actions of 1960 and the larger attacks (a few of battalion size) of 1961 were also not organized by the NLF—which did not exist until the last days of 1960 and was hardly an effective organization ready to launch full-scale guerrilla warfare in 1961—it appears that it was strength in the South, not weakness, which triggered the formation of the NLF.

In spite of this evidence, some contend that the NLF was a totally indigenous Southern creation.[14] It is argued by its present chairman that its origins go back to the Saigon-Cholon Peace Committee of 1954 and that it expresses the revolutionary desire of the peoples of the South. The formal organization of the NLF in South Vietnam was carried out by a very small group of Southerners—perhaps fifty or sixty persons. Nguyen Huu Tho, a Paris-trained lawyer from Saigon, was one of the leaders and was elected Chairman, while Phung Van Cung, a physician and ex-member of the Diem regime, was named Secretary General—probably the most powerful position. Cung was succeeded by Nguyen Van Hieu, a propagandist; Tran Buu Kien, a lawyer, followed; and finally came Huynh Tan Phat, an architect. (It was reported in March, 1967, that Phat had become the leader of the NLF; what this means is not entirely clear.) Other leading members included Le Van Tha, a radio engineer from Saigon; Joseph Maui Ho Hue Ba, listed as a Catholic and professor; and Ho Thu, a pharmacist. It is interesting to note that many of the leaders were well educated and lived in Saigon. The top leadership hardly came from the peasantry, though it does appear to understand their grievances and to develop appeals for their support. There were also representatives of the old Vietminh revolutionaries; e.g., Vo Chi Cong, from Quang Nam; Nguyen Thi Dinh, a peasant from Ben Tre; and Ami Doan, a *montagnard* woman from Cheo Reo.[15] The NLF's known leaders are all Southern, but the impetus for its creation and the organizational concept came from Hanoi.

At first, however, the NLF was little more than a front for a few weak organizations and groups. Small, inconsequential organizations of the ethnic minorities, peasants, students, and dissident political leaders were represented.

It was intended that more organizations would join the Front and openings at the top of the organization were left for the potential members as an inducement for them. With the organizational talent available—Southerners trained in the North, Vietminh, and a few Northern cadres—the Communists were able slowly but surely to develop not only the NLF itself, but also the associated mass groups to support it. While the Communists did not deliberately hide their sponsorship of the NLF, they initially took some pains to stress the broad nature of the Front and to play down their own role in it. But it is abundantly clear from interrogation of Viet Cong prisoners that the NLF is the tool of the Communists, who direct its every move.

The newly formed NLF announced a broad, uncontroversial ten-point program, which has remained the basic statement of its goals. It called for a coalition government—although in fact the leadership has usually refused to accept the G.V.N. as a participating member—democracy, development of the economy, and greater education. The program provided for adequate armed forces and the protection of minority rights and advocated nonalignment in foreign policy (although the D.R.V.N. was considered to be in a special category, not covered by this phrase). Re-unification was an important point, but one about which the NLF has vacillated to some extent. Finally, the program condemned war. This program—like the organization itself—was admirably devised to attract a large following.

The National Liberation Front serves many purposes for the Communists. It represented a broad national front to which all opponents of Diem were expected to rally, and it has continued to provide a base for anti-G.V.N. elements. It was the Communist hope that the intellectuals, the peasants, members of the sects, and the ethnic minorities, as well as new dissidents, could all find something for themselves in its broad program. Second, by gathering all groups in one organization, it is easier for the Communists to manipulate them and often to play them off against each other. Third, the NLF brings together some of the natural dissident leaders and so provides a base for Communist recruiting. Finally, it was hoped that the Front would provide the basis for a future government. The NLF has representatives in a few foreign countries and takes the line that the Saigon government is the illegal one, that the NLF reflects the true aspirations of the Vietnamese people.

On January 1, 1962, little more than a year after the announcement of the formation of the NLF, the Communists announced the formation of the People's Revolutionary Party (PRP), an admittedly Communist Party, which "became a member" and has always been the guiding force of the NLF. It is not clear why Hanoi chose this time to announce the PRP, for the Front was successfully representing itself as a non-Communist organization opposing Diem. Some observers, assuming that the South wing of the Lao Dong was ineffective, believe the Communists wanted to strengthen the NLF with a Communist Party backbone, to give a more ideological slant to the revolution, and to provide moral support to the Communists in the South.[16]

However, given the frail nature of the NLF in January, 1962, *and* the fact that the war was going well for the insurgents (both the G.V.N. and the United States became very disturbed in 1961, as witnessed by both Eugene Staley's and General Maxwell Taylor's missions to South Vietnam during the year), it is more likely that by this time the Communists felt confident enough to organize openly a Communist Party. Even more important, they probably wished to emphasize the Southern nature of the insurgency, and therefore set up an allegedly independent Southern party that admitted only the usual Communist relationships with the Lao Dong Party in the North. The party was "formed" with great rapidity and skill, again revealing that it was more of a change of name than the creation of a new party.

Even this openly Communist Party did not stress its Communist goals. In its ten-point program, most of the NLF goals were repeated, but there was a much stronger emphasis on anti-Americanism. Three of the ten points were to abolish the U.S. economic monopoly, eliminate U.S. cultural enslavement, and terminate the American adviser system and bases. As time went on, some Communist goals were added to the nationalistic ones, and in most cases the cadres announced that the plan was eventually to introduce a socialist society in South Vietnam. However, the first major objectives remained the overthrow of Diem and his successors and the ejection of the Americans.

The Communists themselves seem to realize that Communism itself cannot yet be understood by the peasants, and—perhaps even more significant— that it is not an acceptable rallying or energizing force for most Vietnamese. In the earlier war against the French and now in the one against the G.V.N., they have constantly emphasized themes such as nationalism, social improvement, and antiimperialism. They have sought to build as strong a Communist apparatus (PRP) as possible, but have muted though not denied its Communist line.

The NLF and the PRP have parallel organizations, permitting the PRP to control and manipulate the NLF at all echelons. At the top of both organizations are large central committees that meet infrequently, but contain smaller sub-groupings, presidiums, and secretary generals with secretariats which carry on the day-to-day work. There are staff sections in both secretariats to deal with organization, taxation, propaganda, military affairs, and administration. The NLF Central Committee is composed of representatives from the various member organizations of the Front, while all members of the PRP Central Committee are dedicated Communists. There is, however, an interlocking directorate at this level, as top Communists occupy key positions in the NLF Central Committee. At each level—through region, zone, province, and district—there is a similar matching organization with the same relationship between the broad NLF and the tightly organized PRP. At the village and lower levels, the organization is simple but roughly of the same nature. In the great Cholon—Saigon—Gia Dinh complex, the Viet Cong have an elaborate organization with a hierarchy similar to the rural one, whose top committees report directly to the NLF and PRP headquarters. In addition to this vertical command structure, the NLF has its mass organizations—the most important of which are the farmer, youth, women, student worker, and intellectual associations—which are means of involving as many persons as possible in the organization and activities of the Front. These associations mobilize functional elements of society for narrower group goals as well as for the NLF objectives.

This Viet Cong apparatus has grown in numbers and influence. In 1961 its successes caused considerable concern in both Saigon and Washington, and American economic and military aid and the number of U.S. advisers were greatly increased. The growing Viet Cong strength also induced the Diem regime to inaugurate the strategic hamlet plan. The program, largely borrowed from the British experience in Malaya, was an attempt to group people into more defensible locations and at the same time to improve their social and economic welfare. In 1962, this program caused the Viet Cong to become increasingly concerned about the great strain being placed on their organization and activities. Although they remained certain of victory, the immediate future worried them. However, their efforts to destroy the strategic hamlets and to discredit the program—along with ineptitude, inefficiency, and mishandling on the part of the G.V.N.—reduced this threat by 1963.

Internal discontent, especially the Buddhist outbreaks of spring, 1963, revealed the shaky foundations of the Diem regime and encouraged the Viet Cong. As the possibility of Diem's overthrow loomed greater, the Viet Cong leadership grappled with the problem of how to take advantage of it. Diem's assassination in November, 1963, turned out to be not an unmixed blessing for the NLF. While the coup eliminated a corrupt and increasingly inefficient regime, it also rid the country of the greatest object of hate and hence an important motivating element for some parts of the NLF. Membership in the NLF dropped after the coup, as many opponents of Diem thought the struggle was over. On the other hand, the vacuum left by the removal of Diem gave the NLF a great opportunity to seize power. The Viet Cong military forces tried, but failed. Viet Cong activity reached its highest level immediately after the coup. While the NLF was not able to seize power even during the paralysis of the country, it did make considerable gains as time moved on and there was no firm hand at the wheel. By 1964, the country-wide operations of the Viet Cong had the G.V.N. tottering. The Viet Cong had nearly achieved victory by early 1965, when American bombing and the introduction of large numbers of troops began.

From 1956 to 1964, Hanoi seems to have played a key but somewhat surreptitious role in the developing insurgency in the South. The D.R.V.N. has disguised and denied its aid, but there is too much evidence to doubt its existence. In the speeches of its leaders and the broadcasts of Radio Hanoi, the

D.R.V.N. constantly stressed the unification theme and the need to overthrow Diem and his successors, and provided broad moral support for subversive action in the South. It has been the guiding force in overall policy and strategy and has made the crucial decisions. Ho Chi Minh himself probably masterminded the formation of the NLF and the "new" PRP. Until 1964, however, most support was of an intangible nature; thereafter, actual matériel and manpower assistance increased greatly. Although inciting to rebellion, aiding and abetting insurgents, and providing supplies may not constitute overt aggression, they certainly represent at the very least interference in the internal affairs of South Vietnam. Infiltration of D.R.V.N. troops into the South is quite another matter and is clearly aggression. However, all of this assistance should not overshadow the fact that there was considerable indigenous unrest in the South, without which there would have been little insurgency.

This combined Northern and Southern, Communist-directed effort has produced a remarkable organization which is composed of three major groups, two of which have been previously discussed. The first is the avowedly Communist PRP, the tightly organized and somewhat exclusive unit which is responsible for policy decision-making and overall control. It dominates and directs the second group, the NLF, which is the mass organization serving as a broad front for the insurgency. The third group is the National Liberation Army, which is the military arm of the organization and is discussed in the next chapter. It is this efficient combination of a mass-movement front and a tightly organized Communist Party with its own army that is the really important threat in Vietnam, as the Saigon government has no comparable organization.

NOTES

1. This broad term, the Geneva Accords, also includes the military cease-fire agreements for Laos and Cambodia, but they are not discussed here for obvious reasons.

2. This brief summary of the conditions of the Geneva Accords is not addressed to the many serious questions arising out of this conference, such as the legality of the Accords, whether the United States was committed, and whether the Government of South Vietnam was bound. Though important, these questions are not critical to the subject of this book.

3. The Dai Viet or Dai Viet Quoc Dan Hoi (the National Party of Greater Vietnam) was formed in 1945 in northern Annam as an anti-French group. It is quite secretive and has members in the present Saigon government. The VNQDD or Vietnam Quoc Dan Dong (Vietnam Nationalist Party) is an older nationalist party which was founded in 1927. It is modeled after the Chinese Kuomintang Party and looked to the Chinese for aid in expelling the French. This group is also active in the present Saigon regime, especially in the I Corps area.

4. Bernard Fall, in *Viet-Nam Witness: 1953–66* (New York: Frederick A. Praeger, 1966), p. 78, states that Vietminh killings began immediately after July, 1956. In *The*

Two Viet-Nams (2d rev. ed.; New York: Frederick A. Praeger, 1967), p. 316, he argues that the insurgency started by "deliberate Communist design" in 1957. See also George Carver, "The Faceless Viet Cong," *Foreign Affairs,* XLIV, No. 3 (April, 1966), p. 358. Ellen Hammer, in "South Vietnam: The Limits of Political Action," *Pacific Affairs* (Vancouver), XXXV, No. 1 (Spring, 1962), p. 30, argues that Hanoi intervened in 1956 because it could not tolerate a better standard of living in the South.

5. Bernard Fall, "South Viet-Nam's Internal Problems," *Pacific Affairs,* XXXI, No. 3 (September, 1958), p. 255.

6. Fall, *The Two Viet-Nams,* p. 281.

7. Hammer, *op. cit.,* p. 32.

8. Douglas Pike, *Viet Cong: The Organization and Technique of the National Liberation Party* [sic] *of South Viet-Nam* (Cambridge, Mass.: MIT Press, 1966), p. 102.

9. Some maintain that the sects did not cooperate with the Viet Cong, but remained separate and concentrated on their own organizational development. The Hoa Hao appear to have cooperated with the Viet Cong until 1961, when they parted company. They then were opposed by both the Viet Cong and the Saigon government, but joined the latter after Diem's overthrow in November, 1963. The National Liberation Front, however, includes some survivors from the time of cooperation by the Hoa Hao and Binh Xuyen.

10. The creation of *agrovilles,* begun in mid-1959, was an effort to regroup scattered rural populations into new centers where they would be protected from Viet Cong propaganda and attacks and their lot could be improved. The *agrovilles* did not work out well. *Agrovilles* were the antecedents in some ways of the strategic hamlets, which were begun in 1962. The major difference was that the *agrovilles* were to be new living centers, into which people were to be moved from their homes, while the strategic hamlets involved lesser movements of people into smaller and more defensible hamlet configurations. See Joseph J. Zasloff, "Rural Resettlement in South Vietnam," *Pacific Affairs,* XXXV, No. 4 (Winter, 1962–63).

11. It has been estimated that there were at least 5,000 guerrillas active in 1959. For one source, see *ibid.,* p. 329. Most such figures are largely guesses, however.

12. See Wilfred Burchett, *Vietnam: Inside Story of the Guerrilla War* (New York: International Publishers, 1965), p. 152. Burchett is an Australian Communist who frequently visits and writes about the Viet Cong. Pike, in his *Viet Cong,* contradicts himself on this point: He describes the uncoordinated opposition existing before the formation of the NLF (p. 76), but elsewhere he says that *by* 1959 an "over-all directional hand was apparent" and that "the struggle had become an imported thing" (p. 78).

13. Pike, *op. cit.,* p. 78. He gives credit for the organization of the NLF to Ho Chi Minh, "Vietnam's organizational genius" (p. 76).

14. Wilfred Burchett has long argued that the insurgency is purely Southern. Phillippe Devillers and Jean Lacouture are leaders of the French school that takes essentially the same line and claims that Hanoi became involved well after the insurgency started.

15. *Le Matin* (Phnom Penh), November 14 and 18, 1964, carried short biographies of some of the NLF leaders. It indicated—even bragged—that many of these leaders had pursued their revolutionary activities since 1954 and had never really stopped. Pike gives more complete and recent biographical sketches of the NLF leadership in Appendix D to his *Viet Cong.*

16. Pike, *op. cit.,* pp. 143–44. Pike is impressed with the prompt organization of the PRP and admits parenthetically that the Lao Dong cadres certainly helped, but does not indicate that there was a good covert Communist organization in existence. Without that basis, the organization of the PRP would certainly not have been as prompt and efficient as he claims.

Chapter 7

THE VIET CONG MILITARY

Although they may represent the most obvious threat to the security and stability of South Vietnam, military operations are, as we have seen, only one of the tools used by the Viet Cong to wage insurgency. The combination of propaganda, economic subversion, and civic actions directed by the Viet Cong forms the basis of their struggle to gain control of South Vietnam. These economic, social, and political actions constitute the vital substructure of the insurgency—difficult to see and even more difficult to destroy. Military actions have, however, steadily increased in significance as the war has continued and the level of violence has mounted.[1]

Like the other activities of the Viet Cong in their so-called war of liberation, military operations are undertaken with political objectives in mind. In traditional Western strategy, military requirements are often allowed to override nonmilitary considerations; Viet Cong doctrine, however, requires that most military operations be justified by definite political or psychological goals. Like the Vietminh, the Viet Cong believe that the army has other missions at least as important as fighting. General Giap, who has played a vital role in both movements, has said that political action is the soul of the army. The individual soldier must understand the political and psychological dimensions of the war and of his actions; he must treat the people courteously and try to help them in their tasks. Army cadres often undertake specific psychological missions to villages to lecture the people on the evils of Saigon and the Americans and the virtues of the "liberation" movement. Viet Cong propaganda constantly stresses the unity of the army and the people, even though each may be called upon to perform different missions in their common struggle. (In practice, of course, the Viet Cong troops are not always helpful to the people. In the next chapter, it will be pointed out that the Viet Cong have recently changed their behavior toward the population.)

In order to assure the subordination of the military forces to the political objectives of the Party, its leaders have employed a number of measures, most of which were tried by the Vietminh in the earlier war. Much of the time devoted to training the troops is spent in political indoctrination. The National Liberation Army and the paramilitary forces include a number of PRP members (often constituting as much as one-third of the total strength of the regular forces), organized in cells and larger units, who help with indoctrination of the troops and evaluate and report on troop morale, reliability, and conduct. There are also Party committees at all levels of the military hierarchy, which lead troop discussions and try to assure adherence to the Party line. Formal control of the troops is assured by the placement of political officers, or commissars (who often outrank the military commanders), with each military unit. These commissars are Party members, are involved in the making of all decisions, and can overrule the military commanders. "The Party decides, the military executes," as one captured Viet Cong document explained the relationship. Conversely, military commanders participate in—but never dominate—meetings of the various echelons in the hierarchy of the political organization.

THE MILITARY APPARATUS

The Viet Cong military organization differs from that of a conventional Western army not only in its pronounced political or ideological character, but also in its structure, which is based largely on that of the Vietminh. At the bottom of the hierarchy are the people's forces or guerrillas, whom most Americans would not consider as part of a regular military establishment, but who play such an important and integrated role for the Viet Cong that they must be included in any discussion of the Viet Cong military apparatus. There are two types of "people's forces"—the village guerrilla and the combat guerrilla. The village guerrillas are usually older men—largely untrained, poorly equipped, and inadequately indoctrinated—who perform the missions of local defense and logistic support. The combat guerrillas are younger men who seem to be promising candidates for the regular forces and are better trained, equipped, and indoctrinated. They engage in small guerrilla operations outside the village confines and are used as support forces for the regular units. Both these groups are usually organized in squads and platoons and are controlled by the village PRP organization.

The roles of these popular forces, especially the combat guerrillas, should not be dismissed lightly. For one thing, their social role is as important as their military one, for they tend to involve and commit more people to the struggle. Most Vietnamese families feel responsible for the actions of one of their members; many therefore tolerate or support the Viet Cong because a brother, husband, father, or even a female relative is a member. Guerrillas perform the essential service of spreading the ideas of the movement among their families and in their villages. Service in the guerrilla movement is not only a means of training and indoctrination, but also a period of apprenticeship during which military officials can determine whether a man is fit for higher-level duty in the regular military forces—and eventually for membership in the Party. In some cases, whole guerrilla bands that have proved their combat value are elevated to the next level in the military hierarchy.[2]

Guerrillas perform important logistic functions and assist in regular battles in a number of ways: They act as a covering force, help clear the battlefield of the dead, and stow the booty. Finally, they engage in limited paramilitary actions such as ambushes, assaults on officials, and attacks on small enemy detachments and outposts in their own locale.

These guerrillas are elusive and most difficult to deal attacks on small enemy detachments and outposts in their home areas. They are known to and are an integral part of the population. They are, in fact, still peasants. Families and neighbors are more likely to help and protect them than to turn them over to the government. Their needs are few and simple and their logistic support comes from their home or village. Most men prefer to join the guerrillas because they are told they can stay in their villages and operate on familiar ground, and thus do not face the emotional upheaval of leaving their families to an uncertain fate. They thus have a superior knowledge of the terrain and people. These are the elements of the Viet Cong that swim safely and easily in the sea of the people.[3]

Next in the hierarchy are the local forces, sometimes called regional troops, which are organized in larger units than the guerrillas—usually of company or battalion size—and are under the command of the district and provincial Viet Cong authorities. These troops are often, if not always, graduates of the guerrilla bands, and are therefore at least as well trained as the guerrillas. At the level of the local forces, there is greater emphasis on unit tactics and support weapons and a wider range of operations. Their arms and equipment are superior to those used by the guerrillas, but are still not always plentiful or modern. The local forces—who fall between the guerrillas and the regular troops in the military organization—carry out independent military operations, act as screening and support forces for the regular forces, and also engage in guerrilla activities. They perform many of the same logistic functions as the guerrillas, and like them, usually remain in their home district or province (and, of course, similar advantages accrue from the fact that they operate in their native territory). At this level, too, there are opportunities to advance individually or collectively. The role and importance of these troops are similar to those of the guerrillas, though they obviously operate on a higher level.

It was the guerrillas and local forces—basically Vietminh cadres with some new recruits—who launched the guerrilla war in the South in 1960. These forces represented a formidable problem for the unprepared ARVN and its American advisers. I can recall U.S. Army officers complaining in 1961 that, if the elusive Viet Cong would just stand still and fight, or form larger units and stop using the ambush technique, the ARVN could handle them—thus revealing the intense frustration such irregular forces can create. These original Viet Cong forces expanded and improved, and many of them developed into the regular forces that in 1964 and early 1965 came close to achieving a military victory in Vietnam.

The elite of the Viet Cong military organization is the National Liberation Army, which has been organized and trained in the last five or six years. These troops are better armed and equipped than the guerrillas or local forces and are well indoctrinated and trained, having usually served in the lower echelons for some time. Until recently, most of the troops were literate, aspired to Communist Party membership, and were deeply dedicated to and proud of their mission and organization. Newer members, many of whom have been drafted, often lack the skill, the zeal, and the dedication of the older ones.

This National Liberation Army, or regular force, though powerful in many ways, is quite different from a Western army. There is a much higher ratio of fighting men to logistic elements in these units because their supply requirements are so small. The regular force has few heavy support weapons and little gasoline-using equipment, and leads a spartan existence. Some units raise some of their own food, while many others get their food from the people in the locality; in both cases, the military logistic support required is very small. Some of the arms—mines, booby traps, and even more sophisticated weapons—are homemade, and many weapons of all kinds are captured from the ARVN. In the past few years, however, more and more weapons and special equipment have been brought in from the North, and this has made the NLF Army much more dependent on outside sources and in that sense, like the North Vietnamese regulars, more "modern," or Western.

The fact that the regular forces have so few logistical needs gives them great mobility around and near bases and friendly populations, but the simple logistic system restricts their longer-range mobility. The limited kinds and numbers of weapons and ammunition reduces the capability of the regulars to engage in sustained or pitched battles. However, their operational concepts are somewhat like those of the guerrillas and different from those of Western armies, which are prepared for prolonged combat and use a wide variety of weapons including airpower, armor, and artillery. These differences in operational techniques and the frequent differences in the *objectives* of an engagement make it difficult to compare the performances of the Viet Cong regulars and the allied forces—or, indeed, to determine who has won.

STRATEGIES

The overall, long-term objective of the Viet Cong is, as we have seen, the acquisition of political power. It is virtually impossible to know with certainty what strategies they have followed during their long struggle to attain this goal, but one can attempt some informed estimates. One strategy appears to have been to create a situation conducive to the formation of a coalition government— one of the original ten points in the NLF program. This strategy stresses the importance of developing a strong insurgent political organization that can more and more function as a government, meanwhile promoting the notion that the Saigon regime is not the true government of South Vietnam. The actual coalition could come about either through negotiations or by the collapse of the Saigon regime and an NLF takeover.

The NLF generally tends to interpret a coalition government as one dominated by its members, apparently not including members of the G.V.N. Some observers, however, argue that the NLF is in favor of a true coalition government. This apparent contradiction may be partially explained by the fact that the Front believes it is already a broad coalition of parties (it represents two tiny parties in addition to the PRP), social groups, and ethnic minorities, and that the Saigon government is a puppet regime which does not represent any important element in Vietnamese society. By blurring the actual nature of the proposed coalition, the Viet Cong, confident that they are the strongest organization in Vietnam and can dominate any coalition government, may hope to gain support for this solution. In any case, in the eyes of the Communists, a coalition government is only the first step toward the formation of a Communist state.[4]

An alternative strategy that some observers believe the Viet Cong followed until well into 1963 or even 1964 is that of the general popular uprising.[5] In this case, the emphasis is on the creation of widespread social unrest and dissatisfaction. As hostility and anger increase, it becomes possible to foment a popular action that is so overwhelming that the government and its armed forces are unable to resist it. Viet Cong proselytizing and propaganda in all sections of society have attempted to create a situation in which such a general uprising could occur. However, this is a slow process and involves the manipulation of masses of people—something that is extremely difficult to achieve and, in fact, is rarely accomplished.

In both these strategies—the coalition and the popular uprising—the military play a secondary role, reinforcing and contributing to the nonmilitary measures by discrediting the G.V.N. For example, the Viet Cong claim that their forces defend the people from the undisciplined behavior of some government troops, and they goad the ARVN into actions that alienate the people.

Characteristic of these strategies, and of Viet Cong military actions as well, is the emphasis on a long struggle—essentially a war of attrition. The terror campaign against rural officials, Viet Cong military tactics, and propaganda all help slowly to erode the willingness of the people to serve their government, to undermine the will and capacity of Saigon to govern the countryside, to reduce the supply of able officials, and to help build an opposing organization. This insidiously unnerving and debilitating campaign constitutes one of the major problems of this unusual war.

While there is a great emphasis on the long war of attrition and ultimate victory, not all Communist leaders have infinite patience. Giap never believed that guerrillas could win a war alone, and advocated the general military offensive as the means to final victory. We have noted that in 1946 and 1951, he opted prematurely for the maximum use of force to hasten victory. If he is masterminding the revolution in the South, it is not unreasonable to expect a great emphasis on the use of force and, at times, impatience with the tempo of progress.

The military solution as outlined and achieved in 1954 by Giap was described in Chapter 1. This strategy involves the gradual buildup of large military units that can eventually take the offensive against the enemy and defeat him in open battle. While warfare in this phase is more conventional than in earlier phases, it is still highly mobile and is waged without front lines.

Many observers believe that if it were not for the introduction of American troops, it would not have been necessary for the Viet Cong to proceed to the third military stage in order to achieve victory. The Viet Cong infrastructure and military forces were becoming increasingly powerful, and their political base was improving and broadening. In spite of vastly increased U.S. military and economic aid and some actual combat assistance in the form of air and helicopter support, it appeared that the Viet Cong were winning and that one great military push would topple the Saigon regime. Giap probably had considerable influence on the 1964 decision to increase the military effort and try for a quick military victory. The possibility of the introduction of U.S. ground troops must have been considered and rejected by the Hanoi regime, which probably believed that direct U.S. participation would never occur, or if it did, that U.S. assistance would be too late and incapable of redressing the situation. The G.V.N. was indeed nearly toppled in the winter of 1964–65, but the presence of so many American troops has now made such a development improbable.

Some observers feel that both Hanoi and its sympathizers in the South have always advocated the military strategy. It does seem that the Viet Cong have all along been preparing local forces and regular units for a possible military conclusion to the struggle. This is not surprising, since most of the Viet Cong cadres have been Vietminh, whose doctrine was based on the successful theories of Giap. The regroupees, who began to return in large numbers in 1959, had been trained and indoctrinated for years in the North by Vietminh leaders. In more recent years, of course, younger recruits have begun to mature and to assume more important positions in the PRP, NLF, and NLA, but they have never dominated any of these organizations. Thus the influence of the earlier

Vietminh experience and the current Hanoi leadership have made the reliance on military operations great.

Other observers, however, believe that the Southerners in the NLF have preferred the political and social strategies described above. Those who hold this view have not made it entirely clear why the Southerners—probably the younger generation—may have leaned to these less militaristic solutions. It may be that, because the struggle is essentially a civil one in their own country, they wished to avoid a bloody military struggle; it may be that they wished to devise their own independent strategy for their conflict, or that they saw the socio-economic and political problems as dominant and not capable of being solved by military means. These observers assume that there was some sort of internal struggle—probably in late 1963—over which strategy was right, and that Hanoi won the argument. The decision to take the military route led to the stepped-up training of units for mobile warfare and larger-scale actions, both characteristic of the final stage of revolutionary warfare. It has been reported that the D.R.V.N. sent regular army advisers to the South as early as the fall of 1963 to help prepare the NLF Army for this new task. In late 1964, the D.R.V.N. began to send its own regular units South to assist in the final victory.

It has not been easy to distinguish the overall Viet Cong strategy, particularly in view of the lack of information on the actual thinking of the leaders in Hanoi or at the higher Viet Cong headquarters.[6] The attempt to create an environment for victory in all fields—gaining the support, or, if that fails, control of the population, discrediting and disabling the G.V.N. and its military forces, and constructing viable substitute organizations—makes the precise nature of the final stage envisioned in the struggle unclear. This broad preparatory effort makes it possible for the Viet Cong to move in any one of several directions and take advantage of favorable situations as they develop. The Viet Cong are quite aware of this flexibility: One captured document, dated 1963, stated quite explicitly that the options being considered at that time included provoking a general uprising, executing a *coup d'état,* going to phase three (the military solution), or entering negotiations for either a return to the 1954 settlement (with elections) or a coalition government.

The military strategy of the NLF, like the overall policies, remains largely unknown—except in those cases where captured documents have provided information. However, Viet Cong troop concentrations and actions have given some indication as to what the military strategy might have been during certain periods. It seems that in 1962, the Communists were attempting to seize the highlands and eventually drive from there to the sea, cutting South Vietnam in half and securing an easier supply route. The highland area, which Giap has called the key to South Vietnam, occupies a strategic central position and provides a convenient infiltration route (part of which is in Laos), often referred to as the Ho Chi Minh Trail, by which troops and supplies can be brought into various parts of South Vietnam almost as far south as the

Mekong Delta. The plateau, interlaced with jungles, highland plains, and mountains, is sparsely populated with *montagnards* who traditionally do not like the Vietnamese. Some of these *montagnards* went North with the Communists in 1954 and later returned after being carefully indoctrinated. In an attempt to win the allegiance of these highland tribes, Communist agents who remained in the South went so far as to file off their teeth like the *montagnards* and intermarry with them.

Had the Communists been able to gain control of the highlands, the plan seems to have been to interdict the local road system, mobilize the montagnards, and attempt to construct a mountain stronghold composed of bases, liaison stops for infiltrators, workshops, training camps, and the usual logistic support facilities. Many observers believe that control of the highlands has been a continuing Viet Cong objective, and that another major attempt to carry out this plan was made in 1964. If this has been the Viet Cong strategy, it has failed, although the Viet Cong reached the sea in south Quang Ngai and north Binh Dinh and in Phu Yen in 1964—only to be driven back subsequently.

Others have suggested that Viet Cong strategy has as its primary objective control of the Mekong Delta, the most populous and greatest rice-producing area of Vietnam. The United States and the G.V.N. have stated that the Delta is the key to the war. Predictions are made every year of a great military offensive in the Delta at the end of the monsoon season, although none has yet materialized. The Viet Cong may consider a Delta offensive unwise, since additional ARVN troops who would then be stationed in the area would interfere with their recruiting and supply-gathering activities. They may even have achieved a *modus vivendi* with elements of the ARVN and may be concentrating on less obvious ways of continuing the struggle.

It is also entirely possible that neither of these geographical alternatives accurately reflect Communist strategy. Those who wage revolutionary war must rely heavily on the support of the population, and are therefore more concerned with controlling people and with breaking the will of the G.V.N. and the ARVN to resist than with holding any given piece of terrain (a traditional Western criterion of military success). The highly mobile nature of the war further reduces the importance of holding terrain, as does the lack of a conventional Viet Cong logistic tail. In fact, the Viet Cong may even find it to their advantage to change the focus of their military efforts from one geographical area to another, while pursuing other strategies which are less geographically oriented.

An overall strategy—not necessarily excluding strategies emphasizing geographical considerations—is one based on Mao's concept that revolutionary forces must begin their work in the countryside, where the government authorities are weakest, and avoid the cities until adequate popular support has been mobilized. When the insurgents have developed enough strength in the rural areas, they gradually surround the few cities until the cities are completely isolated. Various maps of enemy-controlled areas suggest that the Viet Cong are indeed attempting to surround the towns and cities—especially Saigon, which the Communists have said will be "strangled like a dog." In 1964, U.S. and G.V.N. forces made a major effort to push back the advancing "Red ring" from the Saigon area; the operation, called *Hop Tac* ["cooperation"] was unsuccessful. However, the Communists have not felt strong enough openly to assault Saigon or any other major city. On the other hand, they may have believed that an assault was unnecessary—that once they had gained control of the countryside, the cities would be unable to sustain themselves and so would fall into their hands. The fall of the cities was not left to chance, however, as Communist subversion has continued in Saigon and other cities.

There may be an additional reason why the Viet Cong have not made any direct attacks upon the cities of South Vietnam. If one is prepared to admit that the Viet Cong are receiving large amounts of U.S. aid through economic subversion, it is understandable that they would not think of cutting off this supply of money and goods until the last moment. This may explain why there is relative peace in the ports and only limited harassment of shipping on the Saigon River.

OFFENSIVE TACTICS

Until the arrival of large numbers of U.S. troops in 1965, the NLF Army and guerrillas were able to maintain the military initiative and concentrate on offensive actions. They followed the usual guerrilla practice of attacking at the time and place of their choice and not fighting under unfavorable conditions.[7] Although the attacks of the regular forces have evolved from very small unit actions against a few individuals to regimental- or division-size operations, they have usually avoided sustained combat, siege operations, and long defensive stands in an attempt to husband arms, equipment, and key personnel.

The Viet Cong have three offensive tactics, the most important of which is the ambush, which was practiced so successfully by the Vietminh against the French. An ambush may serve a variety of purposes. One of the foremost goals, as in many other Viet Cong activities, is to discredit and undermine the position of the Saigon government. The fact that the government cannot provide continuing protection and is unable to keep the roads open for normal commerce, to prevent assaults on trains, and to stop the mining and blockage of canals convinces the peasant that it is powerless. Furthermore, the psychological effect on ARVN units is that they are reluctant to move out of their bases and thus tend to become static and ineffectual. Not only do these ambushes have a psychological impact on both peasants and ARVN troops, but they actually halt, delay, and make more difficult and expensive the delivery of supplies, the conduct of business, and travel by citizens and officials. If carried out frequently in a given area, such attacks can render a city or region inaccessible except by air—a means of travel not available to most private Vietnamese.

Particularly in the earlier phases of the war, ambushes were often used to obtain weapons. Outposts manned by local G.V.N. forces and convoys accompanied by small detachments from ARVN were fair game and usually yielded a number of weapons, ammunition, a few radios, and other supplies. Villagers could be engaged or forced to stand close by and help gather up the loot. The ambush may also be used to prevent reinforcements from coming to the assistance of a beleaguered post or village; in fact, this tactic is so successful that the Viet Cong often attack villages merely to provoke the sending of reinforcements or relief columns that they can then ambush.

The Viet Cong ambushes may be directed against a single official, civilians traveling on the highways or canals, trains, military units, convoys, or even helicopters. Good tactical intelligence and an excellent understanding of the psychology and habits of the enemy provide the basis for a successful ambush. Intelligence may be drawn from good reconnaissance, leaks from the loose talk of troops, agents within ARVN or the South Vietnamese Government, or interception of U.S. or G.V.N. radio. In many cases, the population provides useful information. It is not unusual for the Viet Cong to watch a mobile unit or outpost for weeks to determine its most detailed habits of changing the guards, travel, outposting, and weapon maintenance, the quality and vigilance of its leaders, and its morale. Once it has been decided to lay an ambush—say, along a highway—they try to select a spot that the enemy will not anticipate. Knowing that the ARVN is likely to suspect an ambush around curves in the road or in thick vegetation, the Viet Cong may plan an ambush in a rice paddy or an open field. Their ability to dig carefully concealed implacements and to remain still for long periods of time enables them to execute ambushes in unexpected spots. Sometimes they will lay mines and booby traps on one side of the road and position their troops on the other, thus forcing the ambushed personnel to leap out of their vehicles directly onto the mines and booby traps. On other occasions, they may stop a column by planting mines in the road and attacking from both sides of the road. There are so many variations of these tactics that it is difficult to develop precise techniques to counter them—especially as the enemy will always have made plans for a quick withdrawal.

In addition to planning ambushes along normal routes of travel and simply lying in wait, the Viet Cong have developed a number of ways to lure or force ARVN forces into an ambush. Sudden firing may draw ARVN troops toward a given area, and they may be ambushed en route. A clearing force may be going through an area and find what appears to be an area of weak resistance; it may then move forward rapidly into this vacuum, only to discover that it has been lured into a carefully planned ambush. If an ARVN unit is crossing a rice paddy, there may be sporadic firing from one side. The ARVN troops will then tend to veer toward the other side of the paddy, where they will be greeted by intense close-in fire from well-hidden Viet Cong. Agents posing as peasants or even as members of ARVN may provide "information" that will lead government troops into an ambush; the same deception can be accomplished by the use of captured radios.

Mines and roadblocks are used extensively, either in conjunction with ambushes or alone (one example of the use of mines in an ambush—laying mines on one side of the road and stationing troops on the other—has already been mentioned). Pressure mines are indiscriminate; other mines are electrically detonated and blow up selected targets. Some of the ambush techniques described above may also be employed to lure ARVN troops onto mined areas. Roadblocks may be merely piles of debris that can safely be moved with little delay, or they may be mined and booby-trapped and thus more difficult and dangerous to cope with. In 1964, an American traveling from Vinh Binh Province to My Tho—a distance of about thirty-five miles—said he encountered nineteen roadblocks. None were mined or accompanied by an ambush, but because he had to be careful in going around them or removing parts of them, the trip took over four hours. Such traps are naturally unnerving as well as difficult and slow to bypass, and they contribute to the general reluctance to use roads.

The same kinds of tactics are used against the single North-South railroad and against the narrow rivers and canals—particularly in the Mekong Delta, where the waterways are a primary means of communication. The river or canal may be blocked, or mines may be laid to destroy or slow traffic and make the ambush easier. But most water transport is so slow that it is not difficult to execute an ambush without blocking the waterway. The Viet Cong use personal arms as well as machine guns and recoilless rifles to attack vessels from the banks. Ambushes against the railroad and acts of sabotage have been so easy and successful in spite of guards, air cover, special armored patrol cars, and other defenses that portions of the railroad have been closed down indefinitely.

To help counter ambushes and provide faster and more secure cross-country mobility, the United States has supplied the G.V.N. with increasing numbers of aircraft and helicopters, which have been used to reconnoiter routes for possible ambushes, to fly cover over columns on roads, and to attack ambushes once they are launched. The helicopters have a variety of other uses as well: They serve as flying firing platforms, transporters of assault troops and equipment, and reconnaissance vehicles. The medical rescue units are particularly valuable—not only for transportation of the wounded, but as morale builders.[8]

The Viet Cong responses to helicopters and airpower have been varied. They have intensified their efforts at concealment and camouflage and have conducted even more of their moves and operations at night. If it is necessary for them to move during the day, they usually go in small numbers, dressed as peasants, so that it is hard to distinguish them from the rest of the population. NLA troops have been given additional special training for using regular rifles, as well as machine guns and small antiaircraft guns, to shoot down helicopters and aircraft. Concerted efforts have been made to strip downed aircraft of their machine guns and to capture these weapons in ground combat. The Viet Cong have been particularly active against helicopters (a problem the Vietminh did not have to cope with), which are in many ways more vulnerable than aircraft. One fairly successful technique has been to entice them into traps or the wrong landing zones. Using captured U.S. radios, the Viet Cong are able to learn of helicopter pilots' requests for the marking of a landing zone and then direct them to an area in which an ambush has been carefully laid. They may use the color or smoke marker requested or issue false orders on the radio. The "landing area" may be covered with pointed sticks and other concealed obstacles, or it may be surrounded by troops who will open fire on the descending or hovering helicopter. The guerrillas have also been known to plan an attack on an outpost in a small valley in anticipation that a helicopter-borne relief force would be dispatched; they deployed machine guns and small anti-aircraft weapons on the hillsides—thus overcoming some of their range and altitude problems—and ambushed the "choppers" as they came into the narrow valley. They have constantly attempted to develop new kinds of am-bushes and ways to defend themselves against U.S. air power.

A second major offensive tactic of the Viet Cong is the harassing, or hit-and-run, attack, launched usually against villages and local defense forces and less often against the ARVN. As in the case of ambushes, these generally serve several purposes, not all of which are strictly military. G.V.N. local forces—like the guerrillas themselves—are poorly trained and equipped and scarcely able to defend themselves, thus affording the Viet Cong easy victories that impress the people with the insurgents' strength. The local troops are part of the population and the impact of successful Viet Cong attacks upon them, often accompanied by propaganda talks, is felt by the people. If the defense militia is cowed by the Viet Cong, the other villagers are aware of the situation and may then be more willing to cooperate with the Viet Cong than to assist the Saigon government.

Among the strictly military objectives that hit-and-run attacks can accomplish are the disruption of possible local offensives, the gathering of intelligence, and the seizure of weapons and supplies, even if these are not of the latest vintage. Radios are particularly valuable prizes, enabling the Viet Cong to intercept calls for relief and other messages and to broadcast false information.

These harassing attacks take many forms. The guerrillas may simply fire a few shots into a village in order to unnerve the people and give them a sense of insecurity. Or several Viet Cong may run from one spot to another, firing their weapons and raising the expectation of an attack. They will not attempt to kill anyone, and suddenly they will withdraw, leaving the anxious villagers to wonder what will happen next. Another variation is for terrorists or snipers to sneak into, or near, a village and kill one or two local officials, making the uneasy inhabitants even more reluctant to assume any role in the village administration. There have also been occasions when the Viet Cong have lobbed mortar shells or projected locally made fire bombs into a village, causing large numbers of casualties or setting the village on fire. If the government does not respond to each of these attacks with a show of military force, medical assistance, and relief for the homeless, the villagers then tend to blame Saigon rather than the Viet Cong for their troubles.

Not only do these attacks create fear and uncertainty among the villagers, but they also affect ARVN and the attitudes of people and army toward each other. For example, one of the smaller harassing actions described above may force the village chief to call for assistance from the nearby ARVN unit. When an ARVN unit does try to come to the assistance of the village, it may get ambushed on the way and suffer serious casualties as well as loss of equipment. If the harassing action is not followed by an attack, the ARVN unit may resent having been called out for a false alarm and having suffered unnecessary casualties. Its not unnatural reaction, the next time it receives such a call for assistance, might be to ignore the call entirely or to take its time in responding. And this is exactly what happens: It is not too uncommon for ARVN to march into a village that had called for help twenty-four or thirty-six hours earlier—when both ARVN and the village know full well that any possible danger has long since disappeared. In these cases, the ARVN has played into the hands of the enemy, and a primary objective of the Viet Cong—to separate the people from the army and the government—has been achieved. The people do not believe that ARVN really wants to defend them, and ARVN feels that the people are causing false alarms and are unmindful of the dangers involved. The creation of mutual distrust between army and people—a political and psychological objective—is thus brought about by the use of military means.

The third major Viet Cong offensive tactic is that of the more or less conventional attack, but an NLF Army attack differs from the familiar Western attack in several important ways.[9] First, a conventional Western army attack is normally preceded by a "softening up" by air and artillery before the actual ground assault is launched. Since the Viet Cong have no airpower and no regular artillery, they cannot carry out such actions, but must rely instead on precise intelligence, careful planning, and complete surprise. Their psychological personnel do seek to "soften up" the defenders by exaggerating the strength of the Viet Cong and the inadequacy of the government defenses. Second, a Western offensive attack usually has as its objective the capture and holding of a given piece of territory. The Viet Cong attack seldom has the objective of securing territory, but rather inflicting casualties and impairing morale, while also impressing the population and discrediting the government. Although the guerrillas do not attempt to occupy a particular area, that area may, in effect, become lost to the G.V.N. because the Viet Cong have so affected the people's attitudes that G.V.N. personnel are unwilling or unable to work there. Third, in conventional Western attacks the assaulting forces keep hammering at the target until it is captured or until they are defeated. The Viet Cong, however, tend to break off their attacks more quickly if they do not seem to be going well. They rarely are so interested in taking or holding a particular piece of land that they are willing to risk serious casualties by fighting a long battle. Even if their attack is successful, they may stay just long enough to lecture the population, gather up a few weapons, take care of their dead, and then speedily withdraw. They have occasionally fought long, bloody battles, but these have usually occurred when their attacking forces were cornered or when a significant political goal was at stake. Finally, Viet Cong attacks are essentially infantry attacks, as they have no air or artillery or armor support. They do, however, have mortars and recoilless rifles, which are sometimes used for a sudden bombardment just before the attack and conventionally as infantry support weapons during assaults. Because of the difficulty of supplying ammunition for support weapons as well as for personal arms, it is usually used carefully and sparingly.

Given the inferiority of their firepower and other equipment, the Viet Cong cannot afford to be sloppy or careless in either their plan or execution of attack. Furthermore, the more formal attacks are usually launched by the regular forces, and they prefer to keep casualties as low as possible among these elite troops. One of the most important elements in these attacks is the conviction of the troops that their leaders have good intelligence and a carefully thought out plan, and have trained them specifically for this operation. The planning for a regular attack is similar to that for an ambush. After the target has been selected, a careful intelligence study is made of it, including analysis of the habits, strengths, and weaknesses of the defenders. The next step involves the development of a plan of attack and rehearsals of the attack, often using models of the outpost constructed in the jungle. In some cases, agents may already have been planted within the village or post; they may try to "soften up" the inhabitants, provide intelligence, or surreptitiously cut barbed wire or give directions to the attackers. As in all other actions, careful plans are made for withdrawal in case of victory or defeat.

The attacking force may be broken up into five major categories. The first element is usually composed of demolition teams or sappers, who attempt to breach walls, cut through barbed wire, or provide means of crossing ditches and moats. Two or three attack waves, depending on the size of the operation, follow. There are support weapons—primarily mortars, recoilless rifles, and machine guns. In many cases, villagers or local militia follow the attacking elements to gather weapons and equipment and haul away the dead. Finally, a covering force is used to facilitate withdrawal—fairly easy if the attackers are victorious, but much more difficult if there is defeat and enemy pursuit.

Most Viet Cong attacks begin at 1 or 2 A.M., rather than at dawn as do American attacks. The night attack, although difficult to execute for obvious reasons, has certain advantages: For instance, there is the psychological impact of troops emerging, shouting and shooting, from the darkness while storming a remote village—or the even more terrifying effect of their appearance suddenly and silently at the village gates. The shock value of these attacks is expected to have considerable effect on the battle—as it often does. Air and helicopter reconnaissance are limited at night, further increasing the chances that the attack will come as a complete surprise. Artillery fire and air support are also more difficult at night, even though flares and other illuminating devices have been introduced.

The assaults are launched with massed troops, usually in overwhelming numbers, since the attackers are trying to achieve a quick success and suffer few casualties. In most cases, the Viet Cong cease battle at dawn and withdraw; if the situation precludes withdrawal, they may "cling to the enemy" as soon as it becomes light, making it difficult for airpower and artillery to be used effectively.

Company-size attacks against provincial and village posts of the G.V.N. (usually manned by one or more platoons) have taken a terrible toll of these G.V.N. paramilitary forces and have brought considerable material gains to the National Liberation Army. It has been estimated that the Viet Cong have inflicted ten times as many casualties on these forces as they suffered and have always netted numerous weapons. Even when air or artillery support was available, the ratio remained unfavorable to the G.V.N. Because of ambushes, roadblocks, etc., reinforcements were unlikely to reach the site of the battle in time to be of any use, and their effect was generally negligible, although when they did arrive in time, they often inflicted heavy casualties on the attackers. The introduction of American airpower and troops, who have been able to engage Viet Cong main forces, has relieved some of the pressure of this kind of attacks, but prior to 1965 they were devastating—and they may become so again if the Viet Cong decide to return to low-level guerrilla warfare.

A captured document written in October, 1964, in the U Minh forest area, gives a better idea of the complexity of Viet Cong military planning, revealing the adaptability as well as the consistency of many of their tactical principles. Designed to serve as a guide for developing tactics of mobile attacks on mobile forces, this planning paper recognizes that both sides are on the offensive in the Delta and that this somewhat unusual situation raises some new tactical problems. But the document begins in the traditional manner; first the planners discuss the effects of the terrain in this area on the G.V.N. forces and on their own. The major features of the Delta terrain are canals and waterways, which tend—according to the paper—to canalize ARVN attacks, restrict the mobility of artillery, limit the use of armored personnel carriers, and make combined operations (infantry, armor, and artillery) difficult. In other words, many of the ARVN equipment and armament advantages are reduced. On the other hand, the Viet Cong believe that the terrain offers certain advantages for themselves: Vegetation, especially along the waterways, is excellent for concealment and ambushes; tactical mobility, short-range, is good, although long-range movements are slowed; and it is possible for large (battalion) Viet Cong units to operate.

In the existing highly fluid situation in the Delta, according to this document, ARVN intentions are not always known in advance, but intelligence improves as the enemy operations develop. Intelligence and the more mobile Viet Cong give the guerrillas the initiative in "strength, time, and place." The guerrillas try to anticipate all enemy actions and moves and plan accordingly, although they are not able to perform all of their usual prior planning in these mobile engagements. To counter sweeping operations, the planners state, small detachments must seek out the enemy and start a fight; the enemy will halt and the "remainder" of the Viet Cong forces will rush to the attack. A special "tail-locking" force will try to prevent the enemy's withdrawal.

In cases where the guerrillas attack an outpost to trigger a reinforcement or relief operation, the most suspect ARVN routes to the outpost are ambushed. Recognizing that they may be wrong about the routes, the guerrillas also plan possible quick moves to other locations, some of which may have been prepared, if not occupied. In most cases, patrols or small detachments try to entice the ARVN troops into the main ambush.

In engagement situations in which both sides are moving, small, lightly armed detachments seek to find the government column, prevent premature or unforeseen actions, and supply information so that a plan of attack can be drawn up and. quickly executed. Individual fire and maneuver by groups in small separate prong attacks attempt to separate ARVN armor and infantry and thus weaken their defense. Withdrawal plans and rally points are planned in all cases. The after actions are similar to those for the usual Viet Cong combat: assessment of the situation, reorganization of the troops, pep talks, preparations to continue if these are appropriate, care of the wounded (the dead, interestingly, are not mentioned in this document), mobilization of the people if required, clearing of the battlefield, and stowing of the booty.

Considerable attention is given by the planners to the problem of airpower. The troops are exhorted to fight airpower—especially the L-19 spotters. Reconnaissance is carried out during the night. Careful concealment and camouflage are urged. The antiaircraft units are carefully deployed and move just like American units—leapfrog, two units in place ready to fire while one moves.

The critical role of the Communist Party in military operations is confirmed in this paper. The Party committee decides whether to engage in battle or not, picks out the bivouac areas, and selects the battlefield and the overall operational plan; the military commander carries out the decisions and works out the details. Party leaders participate in the battle, follow it carefully and closely, give orders, and rally the troops.

Problems are admitted—implicitly and explicitly. Airpower, already mentioned, is one problem openly addressed. The guerrillas also recognize that their intelligence is not always perfect in mobile warfare, and that they may be surprised. Patrols must attempt to fill this information gap and report their findings quickly to higher headquarters. Additionally, there is the difficulty of proper allocation of the limited heavy weapons support, especially after a strong assault when smaller units must protect the withdrawal of the main forces by continued firing. Inferiority in artillery and armor does worry the Viet Cong, although they claim that it is far less important than troop indoctrination and morale.

Throughout this document, it is clear that the Communist planners try to provide maximum guidance for their operating units, in whatever circumstances, and that they are constantly attempting to improve their tactics and overcome new problems. The Viet Cong feel very strongly that they must retain the initiative—that if they are to maintain the momentum of the revolution, they dare not give the impression that they are standing still or losing ground. This does not necessarily mean, as will be shown in the following chapter, that they must maintain a formal military offensive; they can stay on the offensive by increasing terrorist activities and small unit actions, which are most difficult to counter and still contribute to their overall objectives.

DEFENSIVE TACTICS

The initiative is obviously crucial in retaining the allegiance of the people, but it is also important from a strictly military standpoint. Surprise and mobility are used by the guerrillas to compensate for their inferior weapons and equipment; defensive operations tend to rob them of these advantages. For a variety of reasons, however, Viet Cong units do engage in defensive actions. Sometimes they are cornered and compelled to fight; at other times, a hotly pursuing enemy may force some of the units to stand and fight rearguard actions. They may also make deliberate decisions to protect certain villages or installations that are deemed vital. There are also political reasons for standing and fighting at times. The Viet Cong have been ingenious and tough in their defensives when they have engaged in them; indeed, they have not entirely lost the initiative or their use of elements of surprise even when forced onto the defensive.

The fortified, or combat, hamlet exemplifies the Viet Cong defense, which seems to have surpassed even the Vietminh efforts. These fortified villages are completely controlled by the Viet Cong, and no G.V.N. officials are permitted in them. Clever and painstaking preparations are made to keep ARVN out. The hamlet construction committee manufactures the mines, booby traps, and spike boards used for passive defense and to bolster and supplement the active defense carried out by the local guerrillas. The defenders place mines and booby traps along the normal route of approach, so that if an enemy column advances and is fired on, its troops will leap to the side of the road for protection, only to jump onto the mines and other traps. Peasants and often children carry out an elaborate warning system. Well camouflaged and protected firing positions are carefully placed to cover all approaches; access to them is often by a maze of tunnels that are an important characteristic of hamlet defense. The tunnels not only allow concealed and protected access to the firing positions and lookout stations, but provide protection for the population and storage for food and military supplies. A hamlet may have many miles of tunnels and underground shelters. Generally a few of these tunnels end far outside the limits of the hamlet, so that the defenders can escape if the fighting gets too rough. Techniques such as leaving deliberate gaps in the defense or firing just to attract attention are used to draw the attacking force away from the hamlet and into a channel where there may be mines or a carefully planned ambush. Usually, the local guerrillas carry out such a defense, but regular forces in the area may prepare an ambush for the ARVN when it departs, tired and careless, at the end of the day.

In Zones D and C and other "liberated areas," a network of fortified hamlets or even more strongly fortified bases makes sweeping operations difficult, slow, and often dangerous. Prior to the arrival of American troops in 1965, sweeps into these areas were rare and usually unsuccessful. Sometimes defensive positions were so well concealed that ARVN would discover little—or they may have been anxious to avoid these installations, since when they did discover one of them, a furious fight usually would ensue, with the defender having most of the advantages. At that time, the Viet Cong had the great asset of these secure bases in which they could store supplies, train personnel, rest troops, manufacture arms, and construct hospitals, and they thus provided a formidable base of operations in various sections of the country.

THE SITUATION PRIOR TO THE INTRODUCTION OF AMERICAN TROOPS

In the winter of 1964–65, the combined actions of the PRP, NLF, and the National Liberation Army had nearly defeated the G.V.N. Conservative estimates gave the NLF control over at least half the population and perhaps two-thirds the area of South Vietnam. Political stability was lacking in Saigon and the government was increasingly weak and ineffective in the countryside. On a visit to the I Corps area in the fall of 1964, the author was told that the whole area "was going down the drain." The only place controlled by the government in Quang Tin Province was Tam Ky, the capital city, and most Americans rarely left it except to accompany the few ARVN operations. Chinese merchants, convinced that the end was near, were not restocking their stores, and rich Vietnamese were frantically sending money abroad or leaving the country. The attitude of the children had changed from one of friendliness to one of arrogance, spite, and hostility. Military maps showed the Viet Cong steadily moving out of the hills toward Route 1 and the coast. ARVN morale was as low as its level of operations. Both the population and the Americans felt the Viet Cong were about to take over. Though the I Corps area may have been in the worst shape, most of Vietnam seemed to be in a deteriorating state.[10] The enemy was far from perfect, but psychological attacks on the people and on the G.V.N. had weakened morale, while the military blows had ARVN reeling. Most observers thought drastic measures had to be taken or the Saigon government would fall and the Viet Cong would win a complete victory.

NOTES

1. This chapter is concerned primarily with the period before the introduction of American troops and attempts a brief summary of the basic nature of the Viet Cong military apparatus. The military effect upon the Viet Cong of massive American participation is discussed in the following chapter. The author is fully aware of the difficulty of generalizing about the Viet Cong military forces, since the Viet Cong differ from region to region and time to time, and other factors make the war quite different in the various parts of Vietnam. For a discussion of some of these differences, see George K. Tanham and Frank N. Trager, "Three Wars in Vietnam," *Army*, May, 1964.

2. There is some evidence that, in 1964, guerrilla units were promoted in large numbers into the higher units, not so much with respect to merit as in order to help launch the third-phase war of movement.

3. Because of the very fact that the guerrillas are dependent upon local assistance and protection, they may be weak in areas where the Saigon government is effective and responsive to the needs of the people. This weakness naturally tends to reduce the capabilities of any regular Viet Cong military forces operating in the area, as they are dependent on guerrilla support.

4. There has been the possibility that a true coalition government might be initiated by a Saigon regime that was tired of the seemingly endless struggle and actually believed that a coalition and neutral government was best for Vietnam. There were reports that Nhu was trying to negotiate such a settlement just before the coup; and there have been indications that the Buddhists would like to create a viable coalition regime. However, some informed observers argue that a true and lasting coalition with the Communists is unlikely. Others hold that a coalition is the only solution to the present Vietnam situation. At the time of writing, there appears to be some narrowing of the differences over a future coalition in the South.

5. Douglas Pike is one of the leading scholars who suggests this strategy. See his *Viet Cong*.

6. Recent American operations have captured high-level and top-secret documents that are beginning to fill this gap in information.

7. This portion of the chapter describes the Viet Cong application of the principles and doctrine previously discussed in Chapter 4.

8. Sir Robert G. K. Thompson is of the opinion that the use of helicopters also offers some disadvantages, i.e., they tend to stop a soldier from walking and thus prevent tactical surprise. See Sir Robert G. K. Thompson, "Feet on the Ground," *Survival,* VIII, No. 4 (April, 1966).

9. Large-scale attacks have become less common since the arrival of U.S. troops, except in the I Corps area; see Chapter 8.

10. As a result of the increased American presence, this area has not fallen to the Viet Cong, but the fighting there today indicates how strong the Communists were and how much importance is attached to this area.

Chapter 8

AMERICAN MILITARY PARTICIPATION AND THE VIET CONG[1]

In early 1965, the U.S. Government decided to participate directly in the insurgency by taking military actions in both North and South Vietnam. In February, air attacks were launched against a variety of military targets in the southernmost portion of the D.R.V.N., and during March American combat troops, Marines, began to land in northern South Vietnam.

There were many reasons why the United States intervened in this manner and at this time. The primary reason—although it is generally not stated so bluntly—was to prevent the collapse of the G.V.N. and a Communist victory. To most on-the-spot observers such a victory seemed imminent. The United States had tried economic and military aid, advisers by the thousands, small units of combat troops who acted as trainers and advisers (Special Forces), and limited air support, but none of these measures had prevented the rapid deterioration of the situation in the South during the winter of 1964–65. There have been some indications that the air raids in the North were in retaliation for the Viet Cong attack on the Pleiku airfield, but that attack could only have been a trigger. The main reasons given for the bombings were to bolster morale in the South, to halt or increase the cost of infiltration of men and supplies from the North, and to demonstrate to the D.R.V.N. leadership that they would have to pay a price for their continued assistance to the insurgents in the South. It was hoped that the air attacks would make the war so costly to the North that they would bring Hanoi to the negotiating table. U.S. troops in the South were to be used to protect airbases and certain key military installations and to provide a reserve for the ARVN so that all South Vietnamese military forces could be thrown against the Viet Cong. U.S. troops also provided tangible evidence of support for the Saigon regime.

In both North and South Vietnam, American activities have gradually expanded and intensified. In 1966 alone, the weight of bombs dropped on the North exceeded that used on Japan and the entire Pacific theater during the four years of World War II. Targets throughout North Vietnam, including some situated very near the Chinese border, have been bombed, and the sortie rate runs into thousands per month. The results are hotly debated. Many observers agree that the bombings initially had a desirable effect on morale in the South, but that this effect has diminished as the war has continued. Infiltration of men has, until recently, steadily increased, though there is, of course, the possibility that it might have been even higher without the air attacks. The U.S. Government claims that the cost of the war has been made much greater for the D.R.V.N., but the bombing does not seem to have weakened Hanoi's resolve to continue the struggle. As of this writing, the direct effect of air operations in the North on the war in the South is hard to judge, but it seems to have been limited. Airpower supporters maintain that restrictions imposed on the use of airpower have kept it from being as effective as it could have been, while other observers say that the nature of the terrain along the infiltration lines and the transport system are such that airpower can never stop the flow of supplies, and question whether airpower can break Hanoi's will to resist and bring the Communists to the conference table.

In the South, American troops and airpower have gradually expanded their role. Their initial role as camp guards was soon forgotten as U.S. troops pushed their defense perimeters out miles from the bases and began to launch spoiling attacks against the Viet Cong who were themselves preparing for attacks. Some American forces have been and still are engaged in trying to halt the infiltration, especially the Marines at the demilitarized zone and the Special Forces along the Laotian and Cambodian borders. However, more and more, the U.S. forces have assumed the mission of defeating the National Liberation Army and North Vietnamese regular units operating in the South. The 1967 plan calls for a conversion of most of ARVN to the primary security force necessary for pacification or revolutionary development, and for the U.S. forces to assume almost complete responsibility for the fight against the regular Communist forces, including those in the Mekong Delta.

American military strategy has been and still is to destroy the Viet Cong and North Vietnamese units through aggressive search and destroy operations combining air and ground units. The main argument supporting the strategy is that these larger and tougher units must be crushed or broken up before any serious pacification can be undertaken. There are just not enough troops, it is stated, to provide security all over the country at one time. The Marines and the Korean troops, however, seem to have adopted a different strategy: to clear and hold, that is, to take an area and hold it until the Viet Cong infrastructure has been wiped out and the local people have been adequately trained to protect themselves. This strategy assumes that providing security, gaining control of the people, and building a sound base are the first and foremost tasks of the defenders, and that accomplishing these tasks will hurt the Viet Cong most. Although there is serious debate over these two strategies (and one suspects there may be a bit of competition between the Army and the Marines), in the overall sense they may be complementary. The U.S. Army forces may be acting primarily as a nationwide spoiling force by disrupting Viet Cong concentrations and attacks, while the Marines, the Koreans, and the ARVN protect areas for pacification—which is certainly the only lasting solution to the problem. Secretary McNamara wants to do everything, and has stated that our current strategy is to help the Vietnamese find and destroy the enemy main force units, to extend G.V.N. control over more and more areas, to proceed with revolutionary development (pacification), and to interdict the infiltration of men and matériel from the North. This is an ambitious and all-encompassing program in which no strategic priorities seem to have been established.

American combat forces have three basic advantages that have presented new problems for the insurgents and have changed the nature of the conflict since 1965. First, U.S. troops have more aggressive leadership and are capable of exerting sustained pressure—unlike the ARVN, which, in spite of American advice and entreaty, has not in general shown the initiative and offensive strength necessary to cope with the Viet Cong, much less to force them onto the defensive. Second, American ground units have tremendous firepower and even greater amounts of artillery and close air support that can be called in if necessary. This firepower is used to its fullest capacity and there is no scrimping on ammunition. Third, the U.S. forces have unrestricted air mobility through the use of transport aircraft and helicopters. Air mobility is not a complete substitute for the ground mobility of the Viet Cong—especially for short distances and in certain terrain and weather—but it does give U.S. troops great flexibility in mounting offensive operations, rescue and reinforcing missions, and spoiling actions.

Airpower in size and scope never possessed by the French in their battle against the Vietminh exemplifies the character of the American forces in Vietnam. U.S. tactical aircraft are able to range over South Vietnam at will, day or night, armed or unarmed, and B-52s can fly from Guam or Thailand on specific bombing missions against Viet Cong strongholds. Airpower is still hampered by darkness and bad weather, jungle foliage, and rugged terrain, and does not always have the desirable precision, but its ability to reach otherwise inaccessible areas and quickly come to the support of ground troops is a critical asset for U.S. forces and a constant threat to the enemy.

THE IMPACT OF AMERICAN POWER

There can be no doubt that this American military power has had some impact on the Viet Cong military forces, infrastructure, and political organization, and on their relationship with the people. The effects of American military power can be described, but are almost impossible to measure precisely or with certainty. It is perhaps easiest to determine military effects, but even in this limited sphere one may easily draw false conclusions. Even under American pressure, the Viet Cong retain a flexible organization and the option of several different strategies. The fact that many of their units may have been hurt in large-scale military operations does not imply that they have completely lost the initiative or the war.

In spite of these important qualifications, some estimates of how the Viet Cong military is faring can be made. Viet Cong casualties, even if somewhat exaggerated in Saigon, are clearly much higher than they were before 1965. There is considerable evidence that these casualties are in fact hurting the Viet Cong and compelling them to take unpopular measures that affect their political structure and relationship with the population. For example, they must increasingly resort to conscription, which was begun in 1964, when the Hanoi regime and the NLF tried to increase their forces in expectation of a quick victory. Forcible recruiting of young teen-aged boys and even of women is alienating the population and demonstrating the need of the NLF apparatus for manpower. However, most observers agree that recruiting—forced or otherwise—and infiltration from the North still provide enough men and women that the insurgents are not yet seriously weakened by a manpower shortage.

The Viet Cong have felt the impact of American intervention not only in increased casualties; parts of their logistic system have been disrupted. Aggressive tactics by allied ground and air forces have rendered the once inviolable Viet Cong bases subject to attack by ground forces in large sweeps, parachute and heliborne forces, and fighter-bombers. The people living in or near these areas, who are now exposed to air and ground attacks, must certainly have lost some of their faith in the Viet Cong as protectors and providers. The Viet Cong have not only increased their conscription, but have also raised taxes and begun imposing food levies on the people. These measures are not likely to endear the Communists to the people; nor do they sustain a belief that the Viet Cong are really winning. The great flood of refugees to the government-held areas may be an indication of their fear of attack, the hardship of their life, and their dissatisfaction with the Viet Cong regime.

The bases are a key to Viet Cong military strength, and damage to them affects the entire military apparatus of the insurgents. When these bases are no longer secure, many operations cannot be planned as carefully or rehearsed as well, and the destruction of food and other supplies may force changes or cancellations of operations. Fewer rest and retraining camps are available for combat units, some of which have been badly mauled. Medical facilities are more difficult to provide, and there is increased illness among the troops and insufficient attention to their needs. There are food shortages because the peasants have left their fields or have been interrupted by allied sweeps, and because the troops, forced to move frequently, cannot grow their own food. Rations have been reduced. The entire logistic system is disturbed.

American strategy in 1967 appears to be to deny these vital base areas to the enemy. For example, the objectives of the large operation in the Iron Triangle just north of Saigon in January, 1967, were to move out the population so it could not assist the enemy, destroy the installations and supplies in the area, and, by bulldozing wide, bare areas in the jungle and destroying the network of tunnels, to make this area less useful to the Viet Cong in the future. To a certain extent, these objectives were attained and in addition many valuable documents were captured.

Combat losses, which have been severe in some units, and the invasion of formerly secure rest and retraining bases seem to have had an adverse effect on the morale of the Viet Cong. After the successes of 1964, most Viet Cong troops expected a fairly early victory. With the advent of the Americans and the increased intensity of the fighting, this hope has disappeared. Prisoner interviews and captured documents give the impression that the fighting spirit of some of the troops is dampened, that there is increasing fear of combat and death (especially far away from home), that malingering, desertions, and defections are up, and that there is less faith in ultimate victory. There are complaints about reduced rations, and the guerrillas feel the cooling attitude of the villagers. However, there are few indications that the Viet Cong organization has lost control of its men or that their fighting capability has been seriously impaired. Because engagements are generally of an isolated nature and there is usually some opportunity for troops to withdraw and recover, the blows are less significant than they would be in a war waged with battle lines, where broken units would mean a break in the line— a more serious matter—and the probable reduction of morale all along the line. It should also be kept in mind that the Viet Cong have usually predicted a protracted war, and that they have been prepared to accept a life of hardship and danger. In any case, Vietnamese life is not so abundant that all of these short-ages constitute as significant morale factors as they would seem to Americans.

Many North Vietnamese troops apparently are not anxious to come South but accept the duty as good soldiers. The trip South is often a long and arduous one which leaves many sick, weak, and depressed, although they recover after resting in the South. Some are not well-trained basically or for guerrilla warfare, and do not feel at home among the Southerners. They cannot desert and go home like the Southerners, nor are they likely to defect. They tend to stick with their units, but may wish they were back in the North. There are a few indications of friction between the Southern Viet Cong and the North Vietnamese troops over leadership, strategy, and position, but no serious rifts have been discovered. The Northern troops still give a good account of themselves and are completely responsive to orders from Hanoi.

VIET CONG RESPONSES

Confronted with the American military presence in Vietnam, the insurgents have had to devise ways to compensate for such losses as the invasion of their base areas, and to neutralize American advantages. Their responses have been varied, and they are in many ways fighting a different war from the one they fought before 1965.

American ground forces are able to bring much greater amounts of firepower to bear in a battle than the Viet Cong. American infantry units have numerous machine guns, automatic weapons, mortars, and recoilless rifles, as well as individual rifles and grenades. They may be supported by tanks or armored personnel carriers which have heavy weapons. There is also the artillery which has considerable range and the ability to fire in all directions from fixed positions. The Viet Cong simply cannot match this effort, either in the number of weapons or in the expenditure of ammunition, and have become reluctant to engage in sustained combat. They prefer short surprise attacks and ambushes, in which the overwhelming American firepower cannot be so effectively used against them.

As was noted in the previous chapter, the helicopter represents a particularly dangerous innovation that the insurgents could not and did not ignore. Hanoi has responded by broadcasting detailed information on the characteristic strengths and weaknesses of all American helicopters and how best to counter them. Whereas guerrillas in the past often shot at the choppers as they approached a landing zone, they now wait until the helicopters have landed and begun to deploy troops. This delayed fire is more effective and— even more important—gives the Viet Cong time to shoot and get away before fixed-wing aircraft can be called in. The Army has attempted to counter ground fire by flying in at treetop level, thus giving enemy troops less time to react and fire.

Captured documents indicate that intense training is being given in how to spot possible helicopter landing zones and how to deal with the choppers when they approach and try to land. Traps and pointed poles in landing zones are often skillfully camouflaged. At the end of 1966 it was reported that the insurgents were placing thin, innocent-looking poles in likely landing areas. The back-wash from the descending helicopter blows over these small poles which, when falling, detonate a mine or explosive charge strong enough to blow up the chopper. Other booby traps and mines are often skillfully planted to blow up choppers as they land. In spite of such measures, helicopters continue to make life difficult and dangerous for the wily enemy.

Measures against tactical airpower include many of those used against helicopters, but greater effort is needed as fixed-wing aircraft approach much faster and carry a much heavier payload of firepower. Viet Cong have been taught to identify approaching aircraft by the sound of their engines. Specially dug holes are used as listening devices, and carefully placed air sentries are employed to give warning of approaching aircraft. Radio intercept also helps. Replicas of U.S. aircraft are used in teaching troops how to identify certain planes and how best to shoot them down. Small-arms fire has been the most effective weapon against aircraft, according to the U.S. Air Force, but the insurgents are also trained in antiaircraft fire, using 50-caliber machine guns, a few 20-mm. antiaircraft guns, and assorted other small antiaircraft weapons. One technique used to protect a man firing an antiaircraft weapon is to build a conical hill of dirt and put the gun on the top. The man is able to move around this pile and shoot in any direction, but is always protected by having dirt in front of him. An attack by two planes coming from different directions will, of course, rob him of protection. Finally, enemy troops do not fire indiscriminately at aircraft as much as they previously did, since they do not wish to attract attention to themselves.

The Viet Cong are particularly concerned about the firepower that aircraft can bring to bear against their own attacks. They therefore stage as many attacks as possible at night or in bad weather, when air activities are reduced or may even cease entirely. They concentrate their fire on the light planes of the Forward Air Controllers, who, as they know, find targets and direct the fire of the fighter aircraft. They tend to deploy and advance in smaller groups, hoping to avoid an attack or at least create a less profitable and more difficult target, and try to divert aircraft from their major attack by staging side demonstrations or raids. In actual combat, they close with the defenders rapidly and often engage in hand-to-hand combat, so that airpower cannot be used effectively because of the risk of hitting friendly troops. These are only some of the measures being used to reduce the effects of U.S. airpower; others will no doubt be devised as the war continues.

The B-52s, based at Guam or Thailand, cause even more difficult defensive problems. These strategic bombers can fly in unheard and unseen, so that the first indication of their presence is the crash of heavy bombs. At first, the effect on the Viet Cong was devastating. They seemed stunned, unable to react for hours or even days afterward. But as they learned more about these attacks, the adverse psychological effects diminished and they were able to bear them better and to recover more quickly. A captured document indicates that by late 1965, the Viet Cong knew that aerial reconnaissance usually preceded the bombers by a day or two, and that the B-52s usually came in three flights in a straight line. After the first flight had dropped its bombs, the troops could run laterally very fast, seek shelter, and avoid the bombs of the other two flights. (Variations in bombing techniques have since made this simple escape procedure less effective.) Furthermore, the document stated, heliborne troops could be expected in the area about a half-hour after the bombing. There are now reports that the Viet Cong are receiving advance information about the B-52 attacks, although they are not able to ascertain the exact area of the bombings in advance.

Reports on the effects of these bombings are confusing. Some claim that all tunnels within one kilometer of the impact area collapse and that many supplies and strongpoints are destroyed. Other reports, however, indicate that the damage is limited and that the Viet Cong have emerged from caves and tunnels to attack savagely and effectively ground troops following up the raids. Some survey teams have reported that they found no damage, and that the Viet Cong emerged so quickly that they had to leave the area without completing their inspection and evaluation. Both reports may be correct, as the defensive installations may differ in "hardness" depending on the terrain, care in construction, and type of ordnance dropped. To date, there has been no careful overall survey of the results of air attacks in the South or North. Such a survey probably should be undertaken.

As was mentioned in the previous chapter, one of the major reasons for the introduction of airpower and helicopters was to make the Viet Cong ambushes less dangerous. These airborne weapon platforms have increased the chances that the enemy troops will be defeated or will suffer heavy casualties. The enemy must make ambushes of even shorter duration if they wish to escape and to move their valuable and scarce machine guns and recoilless rifles before the air support arrives. They must also be more careful to dig positions in the ambush, provide cover, and prepare escape trenches and tunnels. Sometimes ambushes and especially the heavy weapons used in them are set up near villages or temples so as to gain some protection from the fact that civilians are also in the vicinity.

Despite the greater risks now inherent in these attacks, ambushes continue and are all too often successful. A December, 1966, report described a Viet Cong ambush of 200 government trainees near Baria. It happened that the trainees had only blank ammunition and no radio—contrary to the usual procedures—and were unable to defend themselves or call for help. Neither were there security patrols to protect the trainees. It is reported that the American advisers left the area several minutes before the ambush and drove within six feet of the waiting Viet Cong hidden in the thick scrub. Clearly, the Viet Cong knew the training area and schedule, but it also seems probable that a Viet Cong agent in the G.V.N. was able to arrange for the issuance of blanks and the lack of a radio. Another example of a successful ambush—this time of Americans—took place in late December, 1966. Members of a platoon on a patrol stopped in a clearing to rest and smoke a cigarette. As they were standing and talking, a few Viet Cong appeared and then disappeared about 50 yards away. Without thinking, the patrol dashed after these few men, only to be engulfed in bullets from all sides. The platoon was almost completely wiped out.

There are indications, particularly as most Americans are learning about this kind of warfare, that the Viet Cong can predict their lines of march, rest and bivouac sites, and other habits. Reconnaissance flights, artillery barrages, and perhaps chopper reconnaissance still seem to warn of an impending sweep or attack, allowing the enemy time to set up ambushes or to fade away. The battle of wits continues as the Viet Cong devise new techniques for ambush while American forces try to outguess them, vary their habits, and devise means of bringing firepower to bear more quickly and effectively.

The Viet Cong tried in late 1965 and early 1966 to prepare large traps for American forces. The primary tactic was to draw or attract troops by attacking a post, and then prepare elaborate ambushes complete with heavy weapons on both sides of the route of any relief forces. The attacking force was also the blocking force and both sides of the ambush hemmed in the relief force. This tactic is often called the double envelopment, or the flexible horseshoe, as it can be any size and can expand or contract as the situation demands.

The Ia Drang battle in the fall of 1965 is an excellent illustration of this tactic, and one about which we have considerable information from captured documents. The action itself was a gigantic ambush, carefully planned by three North Vietnamese regiments. The action was triggered by the 33rd Regiment's attack on Plei Me, which led to the dispatch, in the size the enemy had predicted, of ARVN and U.S. relief forces. These were skillfully drawn toward the Cambodian border and the trap. The 66th Regiment acted as a blocking force along the border, to the east, while the 32nd Regiment was the ambushing unit on the north. The 33rd withdrew and formed the southern flank of the ambush, thus creating the "U" into which American forces advanced. The enemy sought to complete the encirclement from the north and south, but did not succeed. In any case, the American First Cavalry Division began moving in heliborne reinforcements and called for massive air support. As American manpower, firepower, and mobility began to hurt, the Viet Cong tried diversions at the Michelin plantation and other areas to keep away reinforcements. After several days, however, the pressure became too great and the North Vietnamese quietly began to disappear but they hit one American battalion hard as they departed. Careful planning, surprise and deception, good troops, and favorable terrain could not make up for the powerful advantages the American troops possessed.

Large attacks, such as the one at Ia Drang, have become less and less frequent because American firepower and airpower make them too dangerous for the Viet Cong. The fierce fighting around the demilitarized zone in the spring of 1967 is an exception. However, Viet Cong intelligence is still very good and often allows them the choice of engaging or not engaging allied offensive, or of launching small sneak attacks of their own. Workers used by the Americans to help clear the area around a camp or prepare fields of fire for the heavy weapons will often leave camouflaged markers indicating routes into the camp. Other workers at bases or airfields have been known to draw detailed and accurate maps of the installation, to be used later for sneak attacks. Indications are that agents often tip off the Viet Cong about large sweeps and the enemy simply disappear, even though they are usually forced to leave behind valuable supplies, which are destroyed. Radio interception of American messages continues to play an important intelligence role.

The small sneak raid, or sapper attack, may grow in importance as large-scale operations diminish in number. These attacks may be carried out by special three-man cells against an American theater or billet in Saigon, or by small cells of up to several platoons, called sapper teams, against an airfield or base. A special squad may be given the mission, say, of blowing up a theater, and is allowed to plan and execute the operation on its own. Normally, the squad makes a thorough reconnaissance and study of the building and its approaches, then decides on a plan that includes the approach and departure after the attack, the kind of explosives and where they are to be planted, the timing of attack, and the precautions to avoid interference. Often an alternate plan is developed in case of unforeseen emergencies. Roughly the same technique is used against an airfield, although in these larger attacks the information on the base may come from workers' recollections or sketches instead of personal reconnoitering. There are two basic kinds of sapper attacks; the stand-off and the infiltration. The stand-off one uses mortars and recoilless rifles to bombard key spots in an installation, as was the case in the attack against the Marines at Da Nang in February, 1967. The infiltration is similar to the urban attacks, as selected personnel slip into an installation and place charges on the target.

The Viet Cong probably are more interested in the psychological effects of such action than in inflicting severe damage to the American military apparatus, although the attacks on the airfields are phenomenally successful from a cost-effectiveness point of view. The sneak attacks create insecurity and are likely to result in increased guards, thus consuming extra manpower. The population may also be awed or frightened by such raids. They are all part of the war of nerves waged against Americans and Vietnamese in Vietnam and Americans in the United States. However, the Viet Cong may believe that the urban terrorist attacks are potentially capable of backfiring and alienating various groups, so that they do not embark on them as frequently as they might like to. In any case, the sneak attacks on military installations will probably increase and there will probably continue to be some sneak raids in the towns and cities.

The Americans are placing increasing emphasis on defensive measures against these sapper attacks. Air patrols, flying irregular patterns and using the most modern sensors (radar, infrared, and photographic equipment), are employed to spot unusual movements or the emplacement of weapons. Ground alert aircraft and choppers supplement this air surveillance. On the ground, passive measures such as fences, illumination devices, towers, dispersing of aircraft, and revetments and detection devices (anti-mortar radars) are reinforced by active ground patrols, often using dogs, special alert units on the base, and extended perimeter defense and patrols. Although these defensive arrangements have been considerably improved, even the most optimistic admit that not all small surprise attacks can be prevented or stopped quickly enough.

The Viet Cong have become even more ingenious than the Vietminh in the employment of mines and booby traps. A few of these mines are reported to be so powerful that they are effective against personnel within a radius of 150 feet. Anti-armor mines are concocted from captured 105-mm. artillery rounds or are prepared by the Viet Cong from captured explosives. Americans do not use antitank mines, as the enemy has no armor or armored vehicles; the Viet Cong are therefore unable to secure these mines for use against American tanks. Booby traps are produced in a multitude of forms, from simple pungi sticks (boards with large nails sticking out of them) to rather sophisticated explosive devices. Americans protected themselves against the pungi board by wearing heavy boots, but then the Viet Cong put bullets in the boards so that foot pressure exploded them and heavy boots were no longer protection. Electrically detonated mortar shells are hung in the jungle foliage over a likely route; when exploded, these result in deadly showers of shrapnel. The Viet Cong also hang old cans filled with explosives in the trees and release them into advancing patrols, or build great heavy boards full of nails which swing across the path of troops and rip into their chests and faces. Psychological warfare is often used to get Americans to "trigger" booby traps; Americans may encounter an insulting sign which they rip off, only to find that the "sign" is a booby trap. These weapons are taking an unusually high toll of Americans: In the Iron Triangle Operation of October, 1965, about 95 per cent of the American casualties were a result of mines and booby traps. Overall, the casualty rates from these kinds of weapons are several times higher than in World War II or the Korean War. The extensive use of such weapons has led the U.S. Army to establish special courses on mines and booby traps, and recent reports indicate that this course, combined with field experience, is reducing such casualties somewhat.[2]

Cave and tunnel warfare, somewhat reminiscent of that used by the Japanese in World War II, offers a serious challenge. Some of the caves and tunnel systems are used as supply depots, hospitals, headquarters, or rest and training areas, and their entrances are carefully camouflaged or concealed; these have considerable logistic importance. Others are used to lure American forces into prepared traps. For instance, the Viet Cong may fire at a few troops and then disappear—but not too carefully—into a cave, where they hope they will be pursued. The entrance to the cave may be mined and booby-trapped, or the guerrillas may throw grenades and defend the entrance with small arms; in other cases they may descend into the bowels of the cave and hope the troops will follow them into the labyrinth, where they can be destroyed. Some of the caves are 600 feet deep, with a number of entrances and passages; even the man-made tunnels have several floors, many exits, and hiding places. These caves and tunnels are hard to detect and even more difficult to destroy.

All these tactics, of course, have been developed in an attempt to redress the imbalance on the battlefield. The struggle is one between air mobility and firepower on the one hand, and guerrilla warfare with the emphasis on surprise, speed, and elusiveness on the other. U.S. forces seek better detection and identification means; the guerrillas work harder at concealment and camouflage. The Viet Cong strive to avoid airpower and catch the Americans off guard; the U.S. forces in turn try to reduce the response time of helicopters and fighter aircraft so that units will receive help faster than ever. At this writing, it appears that the U.S. forces have reduced but not eliminated large-scale enemy actions; the Viet Cong seem to realize that they cannot launch large-scale operations or maintain large units in combat for long periods without heavy casualties—but they may be willing to do so in certain cases.

VIET CONG STRATEGIC ALTERNATIVES

If the Viet Cong cannot find the answer in tactical changes then they undoubtedly will turn—or perhaps have already turned—to major modifications of strategy. Since 1964, the Viet Cong had been moving from guerrilla warfare to mobile warfare by large units, or the third phase of revolutionary war, just as the Vietminh had done against the French. This development has apparently been interrupted, if not entirely halted, by the American buildup. If mobile warfare seems to be failing, as even the Viet Cong appear to admit, what major alternatives are open to the Communists?

Because it is important to keep up the momentum of the revolution, Hanoi and the NLF could decide to continue or, perhaps more accurately, to resume large-scale offensives in the belief that outside factors may come to their aid before casualties force them to stop. They might decide to accept the level of casualties being suffered, if they could continue to inflict such casualties on U.S. troops that America might not be willing to tolerate them month after month. World opinion and domestic opposition to the war might eventually force the Americans to desist, even though they might be winning in a strictly military sense. In order to continue large-scale offensives, Hanoi, with aid from the Soviet Union and other Communist countries, might introduce more modern weapons and even airpower into the war. A few surprise, perhaps kamikaze, raids on eight or ten airfields would seriously reduce U.S. airpower, at least temporarily. However, such raids would not alter the basic imbalance in firepower, and would involve not only a serious escalation of the war by Hanoi, but a massive involvement (however indirect) of other Communist countries, and this seems unlikely. Even if Hanoi tries to introduce more modern weapons, the United States would be more likely to give up the struggle because of a variety of domestic and international pressures than because of such escalation, and there remains the possibility that the United States might in turn escalate its effort.

It is also possible that the Communists may continue to maintain both the large NLA units and the Northern regulars, but conceal and scatter them in order to keep the U.S. forces occupied in searching for these units or anticipating enemy ambush or attack. The American military then cannot participate adequately in the constructive phase of the war—the pacification effort—or break up into smaller units to track down the guerrillas. In order to make this strategy work, the Viet Cong will have to attack in large units occasionally and will have to make certain that the Americans know there are large units in existence.[3] They might eventually be able to achieve some victories by surprise attacks on American troops who become bored or too relaxed by the quiet war. This strategy also has the advantage of not disbanding the large units, which might be construed by the soldiers or the people as a step backward. The decision to disperse but not disband large units could inaugurate a long war of attrition, largely carried on by guerrillas and the political infrastructure of the NLF. Before choosing such a strategy, the Viet Cong must decide whether the large units could survive a determined and prolonged American effort to seek and destroy them, and whether the NLF guerrilla and political organization could continue its underground efforts under these circumstances. The present enemy answers to both questions seem to be affirmative.

A third and more drastic possibility is for the Communists to cease all attempts at large-scale warfare, disband their units and perhaps even send the Northern ones home, and return entirely to guerrilla, terroristic, and political warfare. This strategy would have the psychological disadvantage of appearing to be a step backward—though it certainly could be made to appear as a shift in strategy. It would cause serious problems for Hanoi and the NLF, but it does not seem beyond their capability to achieve this transformation. This strategy has the additional disadvantage for the Viet Cong of allowing U.S. forces to seek the guerrillas in small units, and to engage in more civic action. It might, on the other hand, prolong the war and make it unpalatable to the Americans, meanwhile arousing world opinion even more over the use of massive firepower—especially airpower—against guerrillas, and the civilian population around them, and against the North. Although it is possible that a prolonged and unpopular war might cause the Americans to leave, the Hanoi regime may hesitate to judge American determination and possible American courses of action, inasmuch as it miscalculated them once before. To give up completely large-scale warfare would be a difficult maneuver for the Communists, with serious psychological and operational problems, and is not likely to be their first choice.

The fourth alternative is to stop all fighting, even guerrilla warfare, but try to maintain the infrastructure that has been built up so carefully over the years, and to continue only the political struggle. It would be almost impossible for Hanoi and the NLF to disguise the fact that this was a step backward, and it would really mean the complete surrender of initiative. This would be a dangerous, as well as demoralizing, choice for the Viet Cong, as it would allow the full weight of the American and G.V.N. military and civilian effort to be applied against their infrastructure. The pacification program could proceed unhindered, and the G.V.N. would have a free hand to rebuild the country. On the other hand, if warfare ceased, the Americans might eventually lose interest and gradually withdraw their forces. If the NLF and Hanoi were sure of their political organization, very discouraged about the military prospects, and quite certain the Americans and G.V.N. could not succeed in pacification, they might try this "fade away" strategy.

The final and continuing possibility is to agree to armistice negotiations and seek to win as much as possible at the conference table. The desire of the American Government to negotiate, pressure from other nations, and the approaching Presidential election may convince the Communists that this alternative offers some interesting possibilities. They possess some strong bargaining points: They hold or partially control nearly half of South Vietnam and have strong military forces there. The Viet Cong's ability to continue the overall struggle seems somewhat weakened but is still considerable, and most of the North Vietnamese Army—one of the best infantry armies in Asia, if not the world—is fresh and ready, a fact often overlooked. However, the Hanoi leaders may be reluctant to engage in negotiations, believing that they were duped by the French in 1946 and forced into concessions by their own allies at Geneva in 1954, and that in the long run they will win the present struggle.

In the long run, however, negotiations remain the most likely possibility. Hanoi could offer to negotiate at any time if such an offer seemed advantageous, regardless of which of the above strategies they might choose at present.

If the recent course of the war is any indication, the Communists seem to have selected the second strategy: to maintain their large units and use them judiciously, and to concentrate on guerrilla warfare, sneak sapper attacks, terrorism, and political organization to win a long war. With the exception of the bitter attacks in the I Corps area, there have been few large-scale Viet Cong attacks for nearly a year, despite reports that units are still coming into the

South. It seems that the Viet Cong are trying to preserve their large units, and mostly to increase the number of terrorist and small attacks. This strategy allows the Viet Cong to maintain the maximum flexibility; in the future they may de-escalate or escalate according to the situation and their intentions. Their large units are still available if international developments are such that the Communists may find it useful to put on military pressure quickly.

If the Viet Cong retain their large units but rely primarily on guerrilla warfare, the situation in Vietnam will resemble that of 1961 and 1962, but with a main force threatening as needed. Such a situation poses serious questions for the United States and the G.V.N. What sort of progress has been achieved in five years? Do we know better now how to cope with guerrillas and terrorists? What can be done about the threats posed from the outside sanctuaries? Should allied troops be used in small units to seek out guerrillas, or should they too engage in pacification? Do we know how to pacify? There are no precise and generally accepted answers to these questions.

In conclusion, it may be said that the American military stopped the collapse of the Saigon regime in 1965, halted the Viet Cong move toward a military solution, and has hurt many of their large military units but has not yet defeated them as a fighting force. The strength of their military forces is somewhere around 300,000 and is likely to remain at that level or even increase slightly during 1967. Some more modern equipment, like the Soviet 120-mm. and 140-mm. rockets are being sent South to aid Viet Cong, especially in sneak attacks, and to perhaps bolster morale. It would seem that a high level of guerrilla war and terror can be continued. This means that the Americans have the initiative in many ways but that the Viet Cong continue to a large extent to be able to choose the kind of war they want to fight and, in many cases, the tactics they want to use.

NOTES

1. This chapter examines only the impact on the Viet Cong military and makes no attempt to assess the overall effects of the presence of large numbers of foreign troops or of the vast use of firepower on Vietnamese civilians.

2. However, *The Washington Star,* February 22, 1967, indicated that nearly half the Marine casualties were still caused by mines and booby traps. Bernard Fall's untimely death resulted from a booby trap.

3. The stationing of D.R.V.N. divisions just north of the demilitarized zone is, in fact, keeping strong Marine forces south of the line, just in case there should be an open invasion. Recently a few units have occupied positions inside the demilitarized zone. Using other sanctuaries, the Viet Cong can accomplish the same purpose in other parts of South Vietnam.

EPILOGUE

The Communist-led revolutionary movement in Vietnam—punctuated by the short, relatively peaceful period following the Geneva Accords—has followed basically consistent policies and strategies in its struggle to achieve complete political power in all of Vietnam. But the brief, Geneva-imposed armistice makes it convenient to refer to the first and second Vietnamese wars, and to note some differences as well as similarities between them, always keeping in mind the underlying continuity of the struggle. In both cases, the Communists started as the weaker group against an established authority—although the "authority," whether it was the French or the various Saigon regimes, never managed to exercise effective control of Vietnam once the insurgency began. Operating in rural guerrilla movements at first, the Communists slowly attempted to gain control of more and more of the people through a combination of propaganda, civic action, and a selective use of terror. Their basic strategy was one of attrition, of slowly undermining the established regimes and wearing down the will of the opposition. In order to appeal to and organize the most diverse elements of society, the Communists formed and strictly controlled front organizations, the Vietminh and later the National Liberation Front.

In both wars, the Communists developed a well-disciplined and responsive insurgency organization that included civil as well as military elements. The core of each organization was and is a dedicated and highly motivated Communist Party, which determines policies and strategies to be executed by the lower echelons of the Party organization and through the fronts and the military forces. The present organization covers most of Vietnam and is probably the strongest Vietnamese entity in the South today. This Communist organization achieves the integration of all means of conflict—political, psychological, economic, and military—and this is the source of the insurgent strength. In spite of the tremendous military power introduced in 1965 by the Americans, this entire apparatus continues to function and to constitute a threat to the security and stability of South Vietnam.

In both wars, external powers have provided various forms of assistance to the insurgents. After 1949, when the Red Chinese reached the Vietnamese border, they trained and supported the Vietminh and gradually increased their military aid, which was particularly helpful in the Vietminh victory at Dien Bien Phu. When it became clear in 1956 that no elections would be held in South Vietnam, Hanoi helped the insurgent movement in the South to revive— if it did not actually instigate it—and has since increasingly provided encouragement and assistance. While the North has attempted to hide these actions, it has become difficult and finally impossible to do so as their scope and size have increased. In 1964, Northern troops began to move South to participate directly in the struggle. Aerial photographs as well as other evidence indicate that the movement of military supplies to the South is at a level of between 30 to 40 tons per day. This is not very much according to American army needs, but it represents quite a bit of support for the more spartan and less modem Communist military forces.

Although the Viet Cong have used the Vietminh organization and personnel, have profited from the earlier experience, have known how to give their goals considerable appeal, and have had valuable assistance from the North, they do not seem to have gained comparable respect or popularity. They have not been able to develop a mobilizing or crystallizing issue that would be as effective as the desire for an independent, united country was for the Vietminh immediately after World War II. The Vietminh, under the charismatic leadership of Ho Chi Minh, were able to take over the control of the nationalist and anticolonial movement and wipe out most of the rival nationalists. This able leadership and an undisputed cause gave them great strength and popularity. The Viet Cong have attempted to revive the anticolonial, anti-imperialist issue, this time against the United States, and have accused the various Saigon regimes of being puppets or lackeys of the U.S. imperialists, but the campaign has not had the deep appeal of the earlier campaign. Actually, while the government in Saigon may be quite dependent on the United States, it is still an indigenous and free Vietnamese regime. The 1966 elections and the promulgation of a new constitution in early 1967 reinforced this point. Therefore, the present war has some of the characteristics of a civil war, although both sides are aided and supported with troops from outside sources. Viet Cong propaganda has not succeeded in overcoming this fact. Whether the massive American presence will yet give credence to their psychological campaign is not clear at this time, but the danger is certainly present.

The present division of Vietnam into two countries has tended to aggravate the regionalism issue, which was submerged after World War II in the wave of national feeling. The idea of reunification, although agreed upon in principle by all in Vietnam, does not seem to generate great enthusiasm among most Vietnamese. Details of how and when it should be achieved are unclear and perhaps controversial. There are, in fact, signs that there may be some tension between Hanoi and the NLF on this issue.

Because the Viet Cong have not been entirely successful in exploiting the issue of anticolonialism, they have been forced to concentrate on domestic and local grievances and to emphasize the corruption and evils of the Saigon government. But G.V.N. efforts in the social and economic fields have to some extent weakened this approach. The Viet Cong have therefore had to interfere with programs in education, health, and agriculture, and in doing so have impaired their image as helpers of the people. As American military pressure has increased, the Viet Cong have increased their use of terror, raised their taxes, conscripted men, and exerted increasingly strict controls on the population. These measures have reduced their popularity, but until recently did not affect their control of the people.[1]

In general, the problems of the Viet Cong are more complicated and difficult than those faced by the Vietminh. The French were a clearly defined and identifiable enemy, but the G.V.N. and its adherents are less so; nationalism and the desire for independence provided the Vietminh with a vital issue, while this same cause commands less enthusiastic support in the 1960's. Finally, the Viet Cong are confronted with an enemy whose military strength is far more formidable than that of the French.

While the military characteristics of the Viet Cong are strongly reminiscent of the Vietminh, their strategies and policies tend to diverge because of the different nature of the two wars. The Vietminh borrowed and adapted Mao's theory of protracted war. They tended to concentrate their efforts in the North (Tonkin), although they did not neglect the rest of the Indochinese peninsula. General Giap developed his ill-equipped and inadequately trained guerrillas of 1946 into the superb infantry that besieged and conquered Dien Bien Phu in 1954, and even more significant than this victory was the fact that these forces were slowly gaining military superiority over all the French forces in Vietnam. The same slow evolution from guerrilla forces to regular troops took place in the South in 1957–64. Although there are indications that the Viet Cong have tried to develop and execute nonmilitary strategies, it seems likely that they have always expected and prepared for a protracted war with a military finale. The Viet Cong and the Hanoi regime, remembering the French experience, probably felt that it was safe in 1964 to move to seek a swift military victory over the G.V.N. in the South. They calculated that the U.S. Government, faced by some domestic and foreign opposition to the war, would not drastically increase its involvement. This miscalculation of American will and intentions has led to the vastly different and larger war now being fought, in which the massive use of airpower, helicopters, and firepower by U.S. forces has forced the Viet Cong to make significant changes in their strategies and tactics.

The deteriorating situation in South Vietnam in the winter of 1964–65 posed a most serious question for the U.S. Government: Was it worth sending American troops to try to redress the position of the G.V.N.? This one question raised a host of subordinate questions and some cruel dilemmas. The direct participation of American troops would be an important modification of U.S. policy, which had been that the South Vietnamese must win the war themselves and that outsiders could not do it for them. How could Washington justify sending American boys to fight in behalf of a government that did not seem able, or at times even willing, to fight its own war? The presence of more troops (there were already 25,000 military advisers in Vietnam) was certain to add fuel to the Viet Cong accusations of U.S. imperialism and of the complete dependence of Saigon on the Americans. If the United States constructed permanent bases for its forces, the charges of imperialism would mount; if it did not, the credibility of its long-term commitment might be challenged and some of the impact and meaning of its participation would be lost. The economic effects—especially the dangers of inflation raised by the presence of free-spending American troops and by the money poured into the local economy for installations and services—had to be considered and dealt with. Few of these problems have simple answers, or have been clearly resolved. The issue of imperialism is being used by the Viet Cong, the Hanoi regime, and other Communist countries with some success both in South Vietnam and internationally. While American-Vietnamese relations are surprisingly good throughout Vietnam, the traditional Vietnamese xenophobia could bring about some ugly situations as a result of the massive U.S. presence. Inflation is still a very serious problem. In the United States a vocal opposition to the war continues. Thus the political, economic, and psychological problems resulting from the dispatch of U.S. military forces to South Vietnam and the bombing of the North continue and, in some cases, grow more severe.

The direct result of U.S. military action in the South, as we have already noted, has been the prevention of the collapse of the G.V.N., a general improvement in morale for South Vietnam, and some serious defeats for the Communist troops. The nature of the war has changed considerably. The Communists have been forced to make much more careful use of their regular troops, and to rely more on guerrilla and sapper attacks. U.S. forces, using superior firepower and air mobility, have launched numerous large and small attacks aimed at defeating the regular troops and, more recently, at denying these troops their essential base areas. Air mobility has tended to redress the mobility advantage formerly held by the insurgents, but they still retain some key advantages, such as the ability to operate at night and in any weather, and to move quietly and in certain terrains where landings or observation from the air are difficult. Intelligence, though vastly improved on the allied side, still seems to favor the insurgents. The struggle in its simplest terms is one between tremendous firepower and complete air mobility on the one hand and guile, surprise, and concealment on the other—an interesting confrontation. According to experienced observers in Saigon, the war could continue in its present form almost indefinitely. The Joint Chiefs of Staff have recently stated that without more troops the United States may lose whatever initiative it now has.

An evaluation of the nonmilitary outlook is even more difficult. The 1966 elections, the writing and promulgation of a constitution, local elections in the spring of 1967, and the national election held in early September, 1967, are all hopeful signs that some progress is being made in the political field. However, most of these developments are symbolic ones and tend to hide the fact that little or no progress has been made in the development of Vietnamese ideologies, a meaningful party system, or national and local leadership. Perhaps the politico-religious sects (the Cao Dai and the Hoa Hao), the ethnic minorities, and the old parties such as the VNQDD or Dai Viet may become viable political forces, but the situation would seem more favorable if there were signs of the beginnings of broader-based parties—for example, labor and peasant groups. Such parties might help create meaningful ideolgies or doctrines and offer choices to the people of Vietnam, as well as provide vehicles for locating and developing political leadership. There also seems to be inadequate attention to the development of an efficient and responsive civil service, which is so essential to a modern government. It would clearly have been too much to expect the Vietnamese to form and run an efficient twentieth-century government—much less a democratic one—in the few difficult years of independence they have had; it is only to be hoped that the present search for progress will continue and eventually lead to good government.

Pacification or revolutionary development, as it now is called, has been attempted in one form or another since the strategic hamlet program was inaugurated in 1962. This effort to provide better social services and economic betterment for the peasant has never been a great success, despite official pronouncements to the contrary. Reports emanating from the Guam meetings in March, 1967, indicate that greater speed in this effort will be sought. Since haste has been a consistent weakness of the previous programs, this new emphasis is unlikely to produce significant results. Pacification includes changes in people's attitudes and behavior, not just the provision of commodities and materials. There has been a great tendency to deal too much with material things and much less with people. For example, there are statistics on the number of schools built but inadequate attention to the number and quality of teachers, who are still sometimes drafted. People need social associations even more than buildings, and there has been little or no effort to develop organizations such as those associated with schools, parent-teacher groups, and student extracurricular organizations. These American examples need not be imposed on the Vietnamese, but they should be encouraged to develop their own social institutions. The Communists recognize this fundamental fact clearly and utilize it for their own ends. If the G.V.N. and the U.S. Government will take the time to prepare plans that would include institutional development, not just construction and building programs, to train carefully and that prepares their bivouac each day, sees to their provisioning, and assures their security.

The commandos move about blindly, guided only by the reconnaissance elements they send ahead. At night, even with sentinels nearby, their security is precarious at best. Physical and mental wear and tear come rapidly.

In addition, they are unable to vary their itinerary as much as they would like, particularly on the trip back and if the terrain is difficult. They cannot escape the observation of the inhabitants and the lookouts, who are able to analyze their habits quickly. They will shortly realize that a patrol on a certain path will not leave it—sometimes by force of habit, often because it has no way of getting out. Nothing will happen as long as our enemies are unable to bring together sufficient forces for an attack. But when this time comes, they will make the best of it.

Patrol action, unwearyingly attempted by military men who still believe it possible to beat the enemy on his own ground, is often rewarded by serious failures; at best, it never produces convincing results.

That is why outposts, when first established, attempt to carry out some external activity, but then pull in their horns and never try again.

For the same reasons, *isolated ambushes* do not accomplish anything. Usually they are betrayed before they take place and come to nothing; at other times, they actually do us harm.

Pursuit commandos or isolated ambushes are combat operations the guerrilla can employ with the backing of the population and when he has a support organization on the spot. As long as we are unable to resort to the same methods, we will achieve only mediocre results, which are disproportionate to the risks run and the efforts demanded from the soldiers.

NOTE

1. One Viet Cong document captured in recent U.S. operations indicates that the Viet Cong admit losing control over nearly a million people in 1966.

SELECTED BIBLIOGRAPHY

BOOKS AND PAMPHLETS

APTHEKER, HERBERT. *Mission to Hanoi.* New York: International Publishers, 1966.

BARTHOUET, ARNAUD. *Le Livre du vétéran: les psychoses de guerre.* Paris, 1952.

BROWNE, MALCOLM W. *The New Face of War.* Indianapolis, Ind.: The Bobbs-Merrill Co., 1965.

BURCHETT, WILFRED G. *The Furtive War: The United States in Vietnam and Laos.* New York: International Publishers, 1963.

———. *Vietnam: Inside Story of the Guerrilla War.* New York: International Publishers, 1965.

BUTTINGER, JOSEPH. *The Smaller Dragon.* New York: Frederick A. Praeger, 1958.

———. *Vietnam: A Dragon Embattled.* 2 vols. New York: Frederick A. Praeger, 1967.

CAMERON, JAMES. *Here Is Your Enemy.* New York: Holt, Rinehart & Winston, 1966.

CATROUX, GEORGES (GENERAL). *Deux actes du drame indochinois.* Paris: Librairie Plon, 1959.

CHASSIN, L. M. (GENERAL). *Aviation Indochine.* Paris: Amiot Dumont, 1954.

CLUTTERBUCK, RICHARD L. (BRIGADIER GENERAL). *The Long, Long War: Counterinsurgency in Malaya and Vietnam.* New York: Frederick A. Praeger, 1966.

CRÈVECOEUR, DE (GENERAL). *Aperçus sur la strategie de Viêt-Minh.* Paris, 1953 (mimeographed).

———. *Raccourci de la campagne d'Indochine (depuis 1945 à 1950).* Paris, 1952 (mimeographed).

DELPEY, ROGER. *Glas et Tocsin.* Paris, 1952.

———. *Nam-Ky.* Paris, 1951.

———. *Parias de la gloire.* Paris, 1953.

———. *Soldats de la boue.* Paris, 1950.

DEVILLERS, PHILIPPE. *Histoire du Viet-Nam 1940 à 1952.* Paris: Editions du Seuil, 1952.

DINFREVILLE, JACQUES [pseud.]. *L'opération Indochine.* Paris: Editions Internationales, 1953.

FALL, BERNARD B. *Hell in a Very Small Place: The Siege of Dien Bien Phu.* Philadelphia, Pa.: J. B. Lippincott, 1967.

———. *The Two Viet-Nams: A Political and Military Analysis.* 2d rev. ed. New York: Frederick A. Praeger, 1967.

———. *Le Viet-Minh: La République démocratique du Viet-Nam.* Paris: Armand Colin, 1960.

———. *Viet-Nam Witness, 1953–66.* New York: Frederick A. Praeger, 1966.

GOELHIEUX, CLAUDE. *Quinze mois prisonnier chez les Viêts.* Paris: Armand Colin, 1960.

GOODWIN, RICHARD N. *Triumph or Tragedy: Reflections on Vietnam.* New York: Random House, 1966.

GRONIER, M. *Riz et pruneaux—avec les commandos dans la brousse Indochine.* Paris, 1951.

GUILLAIN, ROBERT. *La fin des illusions: notes d'Indochine, Février–Juillet 1954.* Paris: Centre d'Etudes de Politique Etrangère, 1954.

GURTOV, MELVIN. *The First Vietnam Crisis.* New York: Columbia University Press, 1967.

HALBERSTAM, DAVID. *The Making of a Quagmire.* New York: Random House, 1965.

HAMMER, ELLEN J. *The Struggle for Indochina.* Stanford, Calif.: Stanford University Press, 1954.

———. *Vietnam Yesterday and Today.* New York: Holt, Rinehart & Winston, 1966.

HIGGINS, MARGUERITE. *Our Vietnam Nightmare.* New York: Harper & Row, 1965.

HOANG VAN CHI. *From Colonialism to Communism: A Case History of North Vietnam.* New York: Frederick A. Praeger, 1964.

JENSEN, FRITZ. *Erlebtes Vietnam.* Berlin, 1955.

LACHEROY, CHARLES (COLONEL). *Action Viêt-Minh et communiste en Indochine ou une leçon de "guerre révolutionnaire."* Paris, 1955 (mimeographed).

———. *Une armée du Viêt-Minh: les hiérarchies parallèles.* Paris, 1954 (mimeographed).

———. *Scénario-type de guerre révolutionnaire.* Paris, 1955 (mimeographed).

LACOUTURE, JEAN. *Vietnam: Between Two Truces.* New York: Random House, 1966.

LUCAS, JIM G. *Dateline: Viet Nam.* New York: Crown, 1966.

MAO TSE-TUNG. *On Protracted War.* Peking, 1960.

———. *Strategic Problems of China's Revolutionary War.* Peking, 1954.

MARCHAND, JEAN (GENERAL). *Le drame Indo-Chine.* Paris, 1953.

———. *Indo-Chine.* Paris, 1949.

———. *L'Indochine en guerre.* Paris: Pouzet, 1955.

MECKLIN, JOHN. *Mission in Torment: An Intimate Account of the U.S. Role in Vietnam.* Garden City, N.Y.: Doubleday & Company, 1965.

MORDAL, JACQUES. *Marine Indochine.* Paris: Amiot Dumont, 1953.

MUS, PAUL. *Viêt-Nam: Sociologie d'une guerre.* Paris: Editions du Seuil, 1950.

NAVARRE, HENRI (GENERAL). *Agonie de l'Indochine.* Paris: Librairie Plon, 1956.

NAVILLE, PIERRE. *La guerre du Viêt-Nam.* Paris: Editions de la Revue Internationale, 1949.

NEMO (COLONEL). *En Indochine: Guérilla et Contre-Guérilla.* Paris, 1952 (mimeographed).

NEWMAN, BERNARD. *Report on Indo-China.* London, 1953.

NGO VAN CHIEU. *Journal d'un combattant Viet-Minh.* Paris: Editions du Seuil, 1955.

OSBORNE, M. E. *Strategic Hamlets in South Viet-Nam.* Ithaca, N.Y.: Cornell University Southeast Asia Program, 1965.

PIKE, DOUCLAS. *Viet Cong: The Organization and Techniques of the National Liberation Party* [sic] *of South Viet-Nam.* Cambridge, Mass.: MIT Press, 1966.

PIREY, PHILIPPE DE. *Operation Waste: Parachutists in Indo-China.* London, 1954.

RASKIN, MARCUS G., and FALL, BERNARD B. (eds.). *The Viet-Nam Reader: Articles and Documents on American Foreign Policy and the Viet-Nam Crisis.* New York: Vintage, 1965.

READ-COLLINS, N. *Report on War in Indochina.* London, 1953.

RÉNALD, JEAN. *L'Enfer de Dien Bien Phu.* Paris: Flammarion, 1954.

RÉNALD, JEAN, and ONG-CHÚA. *Ho Chi Minh, Abd-El-Krem et Cie.* Paris, 1949.

RIESSEN, RENÉ. *Jungle Mission.* New York: Thomas Y. Crowell, 1957.

ROY, JULES. *Batailles dans la Rizière.* Paris: Gallimard, 1953.

―――. *The Battle of Dien Bien Phu.* New York: Harper & Row, 1965.

SABATTIER, G. *Le destin d'Indochine: Souvenir et documents, 1941–1951.* Paris: Librairie Plon, 1952.

SAINTENY, JEAN. *Histoire d'une paix manquée.* Paris: Amiot Dumont, 1953.

SCIGLIANO, ROBERT G. *South Vietnam: Nation Under Stress.* Boston: Houghton Mifflin, 1963.

SHAPLEN, ROBERT. *The Lost Revolution: The U.S. in Vietnam.* New York: Harper & Row, 1965.

STAROBIN, JOSEPH R. *Viet-Nam Fights for Freedom.* London, 1953.

TANHAM, GEORGE K., *et al. War Without Guns: American Civilians in Rural Vietnam.* New York: Frederick A. Praeger, 1966.

THOMPSON, SIR ROBERT G. K. *Defeating Communist Insurgency: The Lessons of Malaya and Vietnam.* New York: Frederick A. Praeger, 1966.

TRAGER, FRANK N. *Why Viet Nam?* New York: Frederick A. Praeger, 1966.

TREGASKIS, RICHARD W. *Vietnam Diary.* New York: Holt, Rinehart & Winston, 1963.

U.S. SENATE, COMMITTEE ON FOREIGN RELATIONS. *China, Vietnam and the United States.* Washington, D.C.: Public Affairs Press, 1966.

VO NGUYÊN GIAP. *People's War, People's Army: The Viet Cong Insurrection Manual for Underdeveloped Countries.* New York: Frederick A. Praeger, 1962.

PERIODICALS AND BULLETINS

Asia, No. 4 (1965).

BALDWIN, HANSON W. "A Hell of a Place to Have to Fight in," *Life,* March 31, 1961.

BROWNE, MALCOLM W. "This is Guerrilla Warfare: Vietcong's Silent Subversion," *Reader's Digest,* September, 1965.

BROWNLOW, C. "Needs Outpace Strong Viet Recon Gains," *Aviation Week,* March 13, 1967.

CARVER, GEORGE A. "The Faceless Viet-Cong," *Foreign Affairs,* XLIV, No. 3 (April, 1966).

———. "The Real Revolution in South Vietnam," *Foreign Affairs,* XLIII, No. 3 (April, 1965).

CHASSIN, L. M. (GENERAL). "Guerre en Indochine," *Revue de défense nationale,* July, 1953.

———. "Lessons of the War in Indochina," *Interavia,* VII, No. 12 (1952).

CLOS, MAX. "Strategist Behind the Viet Cong," *The New York Times Magazine,* August 16, 1964.

CORTHEU, A. "As a British Observer Reports the War: Weapons in Daily Use," *The New Republic,* April 17, 1965.

CROCKER, H. E. (LIEUTENANT COLONEL). "Indo-China—An Appreciation," *Army Quarterly,* April, 1953.

DRISCOLL, J. J. (COLONEL). "The Indo-China War—A French Dilemma," *Air Force Magazine,* January, 1953.

DUCKWORTH, J. W. (FLIGHT LIEUTENANT). "The Portent in South-east Asia: The Fate of Indo-China," *Air Power,* January, 1956.

DUDMAN, R. "Rules They Use in Vietnam," *The New Republic,* June 12, 1965.

DURDIN, PEGGY. "The Grim Lesson of Laos," *The New York Times Magazine,* May 21,1961.

———. "The Shadowy Leader of the Viet Minh," *The New York Times Magazine,* May 9, 1954.

FALL, BERNARD B. "Indochina, The Last Year of the War: Communist Organization and Tactics," *Military Review,* October, 1956.

———. "Indochina, The Last Year of the War: The Navarre Plan," *Military Review,* December, 1956.

———. "Indochina—The Seven-Year Dilemma," *Military Review,* October, 1953.

———. "The Laos Tangle," *International Journal,* Spring, 1961.

———. "South Viet-Nam's Internal Problems," *Pacific Affairs* (Vancouver), XXXI, No. 3 (September, 1958).

FITCH, M. (LIEUTENANT COLONEL). "The RCAMG in Indo-China," *Canadian Army Journal,* January, 1956.

Fortune, April, 1967.

GROSE, PETER. "Vietcong's Shadow Government in the South," *The New York Times Magazine,* January 24, 1965.

HALBERSTAM, DAVID. "Portrait of Two Soldiers," *The New York Times Magazine,* January 5, 1964.

HAMMER, ELLEN J. "South Vietnam: The Limits of Political Action," *Pacific Affairs,* XXXV, No. 1 (Spring, 1962).

HOGARD, J. "Guerre révolutionnaire et pacification," *Revue militaire d'information,* January, 1957.

———. "Indochine '53," Supplement to *Forces aériennes françaises,* No. 87 (April, 1953).

JONAS, ANNE M., and TANHAM, GEORGE K. "Laos: A Phase in Cyclic Regional Revolution," *Orbis,* Spring, 1961.

KARNOW, STANLEY. "This Is Our Enemy: Vietcong Guerrilla," *The Saturday Evening Post,* August 22, 1964.

KOCH, H. G. (CAPTAIN). "Terrain Tailors Tactics in Indochina," *Army Combat Forces Journal,* April, 1954.

LACOUTURE, JEAN. "Military Situation in Vietnam," *The New Republic,* May 22, 1965.

———. "Viet Cong: Who Are They, What Do They Want?" *The New Republic,* March 4, 1965.

LANGGUTH, J. "Ambush! Success of Vietcong," *The New York Times Magazine,* June 27, 1965.

LINEBARGER, PAUL M. A. (MAJOR). "Indochina—The Bleeding War," *Army Combat Forces Journal,* March, 1951.

MARTIN, H. "Guérilla, guerre en surface, guerre révolutionnaire," *Revue militaire d'information,* August, 1957.

MARTIN, N. E. (LIEUTENANT COLONEL) . "Dien Bien Phu and the Future Operations," *Military Review,* June, 1956.

PENCHENIER, G. "Close-up of the Viet Cong in Their Jungle," *The New York Times Magazine,* September 13, 1964.

PRESTAT (CAPTAIN). "La Guerre psychologique en Indochine: ses opérations et ses résultats," text of a lecture delivered on September 14, 1955, in a course on psychological warfare given at Boblingen (mimeographed).

PROSSER, LAMAR (MAJOR). "The Bloody Lessons of Indochina," *Army Combat Forces Journal,* June, 1955.

RIGG, R. (LIEUTENANT COLONEL). "Red Parallel: Tactics of Ho and Mao," *Army Combat Forces Journal,* January, 1955.

ROSE, J. A. "The Elusive Viet Cong," *The New Republic,* May 4, 1964.

SANDERS, S. W. "Can the U.S. Win in Vietnam?" *U.S. News & World Report,* January 11, 1965.

———. "Vietnam Revisited: Changes in the War as Seen by a Veteran Observer," *U.S. News & World Report,* March 6, 1967.

SHEEHAN, S. "Reporter at Large: the Enemy," *The New Yorker,* September 10, 1966.

SOCHUREK, H. "Slow Train Through Viet Nam's War," *National Geographic Magazine,* May 8, 1964.

SPARGO, L., *et al.* "Probing Viet Cong Strongholds," *Aviation Week,* July 12, 1965.

STEINER, H. A. "Viet-Nam: Civil War Again?" *The New Republic,* July 18, 1955.

TANHAM, GEORGE K., and TRAGER, FRANK N. "Three Wars in Vietnam," *Army,* May, 1964.

THOMPSON, SIR ROBERT G. K. "Feet on the Ground," *Survival,* VIII, No. 4 (April, 1966).

———. "Vietnam's Gains Spur Red Terror," *Business Week,* July 18, 1959.

WARNER, DENIS. "Borders Are Dissolved," *The New Republic,* November 28, 1960.

———. "Cautionary Reports on Laos: Developments Along the Ho Chi Minh Trail," *The Reporter,* December 2, 1965.

———. "Getting to Know the Enemy," *The Reporter,* December 30, 1965.

———. "Indo-China: Have We Learned the Lessons of War?" *The New Republic,* December 14, 1959.

———. "Price of Victory: Vietcong Manpower and Materials Infiltration Methods," *The Reporter,* December 16, 1965.

ZASLOFF, JOSEPH J. "Rural Resettlement in South Vietnam: The Agroville Program," *Pacific Affairs,* XXXV, No. 4 (Winter, 1962–63).

INDEX

About The Author

GEORGE K. TANHAM (1922–2003) graduated from Princeton University, served as an artillery officer in Europe during World War II, and then earned a doctorate in history and political science at Stanford. He taught military history at the California Institute of Technology where became a tenured professor and master of student houses. Dr. Tanham spent most of his career with the RAND Corporation, serving as the corporate vice president in charge of the Washington office. Dr. Tanham managed rural development efforts in Vietnam for the U.S. Agency for International Development, a program designed to pacify the countryside. Afterward he was special assistant for counterinsurgency at the U.S. Embassy in Bangkok, coordinating a campaign to defeat Chinese-inspired guerrillas in Thailand, an experience he recounted in *Trial in Thailand*. Among his other books are *Securing India: Strategic Thought and Practice* and *Islam and Conflict Resolution: Theories and Practice*.